Reference and Reflexivity

Reference and Reflexivity

❧

John Perry

CSLI
PUBLICATIONS
Center for the Study of
Language and Information
Stanford, California

Copyright © 2001
CSLI Publications
Center for the Study of Language and Information
Leland Stanford Junior University
Printed in the United States
05 04 03 02 01   1 2 3 4 5

Library of Congress Cataloging-in-Publication Data

Perry, John, 1943–
  Reference and reflexivity / by John Perry.
      p.   cm. -- (Studies in constraint-based lexicalism)
  Includes bibliographical references and index.
  ISBN 1-57586-309-X (alk. paper) -- ISBN 1-57586-310-3
  (pbk. : alk. paper)
    1. Meaning (Philosophy) 2. Reference (Philosophy)
  3. Reflection (Philosophy)
  4. Semantics (Philosophy)
  I. Title.

B105.M4 P475 2001
121'.68--dc21

                                             2001028969

Please visit our web site at
http://cslipublications.stanford.edu/
for comments on this and other titles, as well as for changes
and corrections by the author and publisher.

To the memory of
MERTON FRENCH
1905-1995

Thanks for the friendship
the encouragement
the philosophy
and Frenchie

Contents

Preface

In this book I develop the theory of reflexive and incremental content which emerges in the later papers of *The Problem of the Essential Indexical*. As I explained in the preface to that book, I see this view as developing out of my work applying Kaplan's theory of demonstratives to epistemological and cognitive issues involving indexicals, my work with Jon Barwise on situation theory, my work with Mark Crimmins on attitude reports, and my work with David Israel on information.

Kaplan conceived meaning as character, a function from contexts to what I call here 'subject-matter content'. The relational theory of meaning Barwise and I developed saw meanings as a relation among discourse situations, connective situations, resource situations and described situations, the latter corresponding to subject-matter content. Both theories abstracted from the utterance itself. Here I move the utterance to the center of things. The subject-matter content of an utterance is one of many content properties it has; semantics is the study of how these properties relate to one another and to other properties of the utterance. So conceived, I claim, semantics can deal with the co-reference and no-reference problems that have plagued philosophical semantics for a century, and provide a rich interface for contentful language to other parts of cognitive science.

If the 'reflexive-referential' theory I put forward is any good, of course, it will have to do a lot of other things, many of which older theories have had a comparatively easy time with, such as quantification and modality. This book doesn't cover those issues. I hope to have more to say soon.

In addition to all of the influences acknowledged in *The Problem of the Essential Indexical*, this work has benefited from recent graduate students at Stanford, especially Anthony Everett, Stacy Friend, Thomas Hofweber, and Michael O'Rourke, from recent work of Genoveva Marti, and from philosophers I talked to in Germany during stays supported by the Humboldt Foundation in the Springs of 1999 and 2000, especially Albert Newen, Daniel Cohnitz, Filip Beukens and Rimas Cuplinkas. Some of the material in this book first appeared in Perry, 1997b, Perry, 1997c and Perry, 1998b.

IN FALL 1960 I went to Doane College in Crete, Nebraska with the hope of concentrating on football. By the end of football season I had decided, with help from the coach, to focus on academics. "You're small, but you're slow," I think he said. It was great advice, and I soon decided I wanted to spend the rest of my life on a college campus, teaching something. But what? Literature was fine if one stuck to novels, but poetry was beyond me. I'm not organized enough to do historical research. Mathematics was fun—but not that much fun. I spilled things in chemistry lab. I loved everything about philosophy—but could one really make a living teaching philosophy?

Fortune smiled. I had fallen in love with a young woman who turned out to have, quite coincidentally, a father who taught my favorite subject: Merton B. French, professor of philosophy and religion at Washburn University in Topeka, Kansas. He taught there for about a third of a century, from the late 1940's until the mid-1970's. During most of the time he was chair of the department of philosophy and religion, and for a good bit of it the only full-time teacher. Mert earned his Ph.D. at Brown in religious studies with a strong minor in philosophy, that included reading through *Principia Mathematica* with Charles Baylis.

Once Mert decided I was a reasonable match for his daughter—called 'Frenchie' then and now— he encouraged me to major in philosophy and to consider a career teaching it. He gave loads of good advice: apply for a Danforth; drive up to Lincoln and take a seminar with Bouwsma; don't just read the continental philosophy your teachers at Doane favor, read analytical philosophy. Read Moore. Read as much as you can of *Principia Mathematica*. "Here's a strange but important book you should try to understand," he said, giving me his copy of Wittgenstein's *Tractaus*. He emptied his shelves of Russell and Moore and Broad and Ryle and other greats.

I was never officially a student of Merton French's, but I did see him teach several times during visits to Topeka, and talked to him innumerable times about our common calling over the years from our first meeting in 1961 until his death in 1995. He was an outstanding teacher, and recognized as such by generations of students at Washburn. I once jotted down three important points he made in a conversation about teaching:

> "Your job as a teacher is not to give a pretty lecture full of learning and scholarship, but to get your students to understand."
>
> "Don't just answer questions as they are asked, answer them as they should have been asked—give the students credit for the intelligible and intelligent questions they wanted to ask."
>
> "There is a time to encourage and a time to evaluate. Don't confuse them."

Mert was a thoughtful intellectual. His smile was an intentional act that didn't merely express an emotion but conveyed a thought: I'm glad to see you; Congratulations; I'm proud of you; Don't worry, whatever the problem is, we'll deal with it. I remember Mert's reassuring smile and hearty greeting on many occasions. Since his death, I've imagined it on many more.

1

Introduction

Not long ago, after a trying railway journey by night, when
I was very tired, I got into an omnibus, just as another man
appeared at the other end. "What a shabby pedagogue that is,
that has just entered," thought I. It was myself: opposite me
hung a large mirror. The physiognomy of my class, accordingly,
was better known to me than my own.

(Ernst Mach, Mach, 1914: 4n)

1.1 Mach and the shabby pedagogue

Mach acquired a belief at the beginning of the episode, that we
can imagine him expressing as:

(1)   That man is a shabby pedagogue.

By the end of the episode he has another, which we can imagine
him expressing as:

(2)   I am a shabby pedagogue.

It will also be convenient to imagine that Mach went on to make
an obvious inference and to say,

(3)   Mach is a shabby pedagogue.

These three sentences correspond to three quite different kinds of
thought Mach might have had. (1) expresses the kind of thought
one has about a person that one is perceiving; one may not know
who they are, or what their name is. (3) expresses the sort of
thought one can have about someone one has never met, but

1

merely read about. Both of these thoughts are the sort one can have and often does have about other people. People at the other end of the bus may well have pointed at Mach and uttered (1). People all over Vienna may have uttered (3) while gossiping about local celebrities.

But (2) expresses a very special kind of thought, the kind of thought one has about oneself. Although in Mach's case all three statements are true only if Mach himself is a shabby pedagogue, we think of (2) as expressing self-knowledge in a way that the others do not.

In two companions to this book, *Meaning and the Self* (forthcoming), and *Knowledge, Possibility and Consciousness* (2001a), I provide an account of self-knowledge of the sort expressed by (2), and relate it to questions about the self and consciousness. The present book is intended to lay some of the groundwork for those inquiries, by contributing to our understanding of the meanings of sentences and contents of statements of the sort illustrated by (1), (2) and (3). We use such sentences to express our own beliefs about relatively simple issues about people, things, places and times, and to influence the beliefs of others about such matters. The sentences are tools, suited by their meanings to express information in different ways appropriate to various situations. I hope to provide an account that allows us to explain the way the meanings of such sentences relate to when, why and how we use them. In spite of a century of attention, it seems to me that the philosophy of language has yet to provide an account of names and pronouns that performs this service in a completely adequate way.

My account should not only be of interest to those who share my curiosity about self-knowledge. Simple statements about people, things, places and times are the bedrock of language. They are basic units of conversation, of literature, of the language of practical affairs. Scientific theory may eschew them, but they are used to report the facts science must explain, to plan and describe the scientific activity that develops and tests theory, and to formulate and justify budgets that support that activity. Logicians love the complexities that come with variables and quantifiers; philosophers of language love the problems that come with adverbs and sentence-embedding constructions. But simple sentences of the sort I explore are the model for the atomic sentences of logic, the sentences that get quantified into, modified, and embedded in larger constructions. If, as I shall argue, we need some new (or forgotten) items in our semantic toolkit to deal with the way such simple sentences are used, the same will hold for those which are logically more complex.

The issues I discuss mainly concern the simple devices we use to refer, that is, proper names and pronouns, including indexicals. *Indexicals* are words, like 'I', 'you' 'he', 'she', 'that woman', 'here', 'now', and 'today', that designate different objects depending on who says them and when. 'I', for example, designates me if I say it, and you if you say it; 'today' designates a new day every twenty-four hours. Demonstratives are a subset of indexicals, including 'this' and 'that' and compounds like 'this man' as well as demonstrative uses of 'he' and 'she'. With these expressions, which object is designated depends in some way on which object the speaker attends to or demonstrates. *Proper names* are expressions we more or less arbitrarily assign to specific objects, people, animals, things, and places, and use to refer to them—expressions such as 'Bill', 'Bill Clinton', 'New York City', 'Rockefeller Plaza', 'David Israel' and 'Mach'.

Theories as to the informational content of statements containing names and indexicals have been dominated by two paradigms, two arguments and two problems. We look at how this cast of characters interacts in the case of names, and then move to indexicals.

1.2 Paradigms, arguments and problems

In the case of the meaning of proper names, the main debate has been between what I shall call *descriptive* and *referential* analyses. Referentialists follow Mill in holding that names are basically just tags for objects; the conventions of language assign names directly to objects, and the propositions that statements containing the names express, are about those objects. If I say, "Clinton likes pickles with his hamburgers," I say that a certain fellow, the one who is President as I write this chapter, likes pickles with his hamburgers. What I say—the proposition I express— is true in just those worlds in which that person likes pickles with his hamburgers. Thus anyone who says that Clinton likes pickles with his hamburgers has said just what I did. I may associate various descriptions with the name 'Clinton'; you may associate others; nevertheless, we express the same proposition, true in the same worlds, when we each say "Clinton likes pickles with his hamburgers." It is Clinton himself, not any description of him, that enters into what we say. In David Kaplan's terminology, what is said is a *singular proposition*, with Clinton himself as a constituent, rather than a *general proposition*, to the effect that some person who meets the description the speaker associates with 'Clinton' likes pickles on his hamburgers.

We should really be careful here, though. Descriptions are linguistic items; it's the *identifying conditions* that we associate with such descriptions that are really at issue.

By an *identifying condition*, I mean a unary condition that only one thing can meet.[1] The classic examples are the conditions that are expressed with definite descriptions: *being the king of France, being the author of Waverley*, etc. I will use italics to indicate that I am talking about a condition. Thus what I said above about Kaplan's terminology might be put better in this way. The alternative to the singular proposition with Clinton himself as a constituent is a general proposition with some identifying condition the speaker associates with 'Clinton' as a constituent, to the effect that whoever meets that condition likes pickles on his hamburgers.

The descriptivist holds that it is some identifying condition that Clinton satisfies that is associated with my use of the name,

---

[1]Elsewhere I've used Frege's term 'mode of presentation' for this concept.

and that is contributed to the proposition I express. This condition might be derived from the speaker's beliefs, *being the current President* say, or *being Hillary's husband*, or *being the man who beat Dole*. Or it might be derived from the way language works: *being the man the speaker has in mind when he uses 'Clinton'*. On the descriptivist view, in either form, what I say may not be just what you say, even if we use the same name.

Two arguments favor the referentialist theory. The first is the argument from *counterfactual truth-conditions*. The referentialist account seems to get these right—at least for a wide variety of cases. That is, it seems to give the right predictions about the possible worlds or situations in which we would count what I said as true. The identifying conditions I associate with 'Clinton' don't seem to be a factor in this. Suppose I am wrong about Clinton being the current President. He resigned over the some scandal or other a few hours ago, and Gore has been sworn in. Then who has to like pickles with their hamburgers for my statement to be true, Gore or Clinton? Clearly Clinton. What I said was true just in case a certain man, the one I wrongly thought to have those properties, that is, Bill Clinton, likes pickles with his hamburgers, and false if he does not. Nothing else about him matters.

The second argument is the argument from *same-saying*. In a wide variety of cases the referentialist account also predicts correctly the conditions in which two people have said the same thing. We need to say things whose truth or falsity turns on the same objects having the same properties, or standing in the same relations. In this case, we have said the same thing if what we each say is true if Clinton likes pickles with his hamburgers, and false if he doesn't. The names or indexicals we use and the descriptions we associate with them do not matter.

In the descriptivist's favor are two problems for the referentialist: *co-reference* and *no-reference*. Suppose I say "Bill Clinton loves pickles with his hamburgers," and you say "Bill Blythe loves pickles with his hamburgers." Now in fact, Bill Blythe is Bill

Clinton, one name comes by way of his father, the other by way of his step-father; he's been called 'Bill Clinton' most of his life, but when he was a kid it was 'Bill Blythe'. We can imagine that some of his childhood friends still call him that, and perhaps some of them haven't figured out that their old friend is now the President. On the referentialist account you and I have said the same thing; our statements expressed the same proposition. But then surely something is lacking in the referentialist account, for these statements, in some sense, express and convey quite different information. To most people, the second statement would neither change nor confirm what they thought about the pickle-eating habits of the President, while the first would. The co-reference problem for the referentialist, then, is that statements that contain different names of the same individual, seem to differ in what is often called 'cognitive significance'. The cognitive states, in particular the beliefs, that might motivate the speaker to make one statement would not motivate him to make the other, and the beliefs, adoption of which on the part of the listener, would show understanding of the one, would not show understanding of the other.

The no-reference problem comes from the fact that there are empty names, names that don't designate anyone or anything. For example, there is no Santa Claus, there is no Sherlock Holmes, there is no Captain Queeg. And yet children believe in Santa Claus, and use the name 'Santa Claus' in statements that express their beliefs, and so have cognitive significance. Adults who don't believe use the name in statements intended to influence the beliefs of their children. Two adults who know that there is no Captain Queeg still might disagree on whether Maryk should have relieved him of command during the typhoon (Wouk, 1951). On the referentialist view, taken quite literally, it seems that we say the same thing when we say "Santa Claus has a white beard" as we do when we say "Sherlock Holmes has a white beard" or "Captain Queeg has a white beard"—namely, nothing at all. For since those individuals do not exist, there are no propositions with them as constituents to serve as what is said in these cases. This seems unacceptable.

In the case of indexicals, there is also a debate between referentialists and descriptivists, but things are more complicated. As with names, the referentialist holds that statements containing indexicals express propositions about the objects the indexicals designate. Thus one who is a referentialist about both names and indexicals would see (4) and (5) as expressing the same proposition:

(4)   I am a computer scientist (said by David Israel).

(5)   David Israel is a computer scientist.

The referentialist view seems to give the right truth-conditions. What David says when he says (4) is true in worlds in which David Israel is a computer scientist. He doesn't need to say (4), or anything else in those worlds; he doesn't need to fulfill whatever descriptions David or his audience might favor him with; he simply needs to be a computer scientist. And intuitively, the person who said (5), said the same thing with it that David said with (4). That David Israel is a computer scientist is just the information that is passed from David to his audience when he says (4), and (5) is the way a member of the audience might pass this information on to someone else, or record it in her notes.

But, as with names, the referentialist has a co-reference problem. Suppose you are talking to David Israel, not knowing his name. If David says (4) to you, you will learn that you are talking to a computer scientist. If he says (5), you will not learn that you are talking to a computer scientist, but you will learn that there is at least one computer scientist in the world named 'David Israel'. How can the referentialist explain this difference in cognitive significance, in the beliefs that might be expressed or acquired through the use of the sentences, if both statements express a proposition about a particular person rather one about whoever is talking to you, or about the name 'David Israel'?

1.3 Has semantics rested on a mistake?

The co-reference and no-reference examples pose a problem for the referentialist on the assumption that it is the business of semantics to explain cognitive significance, or at least provide the materials to explain it. The assumption that this is part of the job of semantics seems to date at least from the first paragraph of Frege's 'Über Sinn und Bedeutung'. There he considers something like a referentialist view, and rejects it because of the co-reference problem. Frege drew a sharp line between psychology and semantics, but still accepted what Kenneth Taylor calls a 'cognitive constraint on semantics' (Taylor, 1995). Here is one straightforward version of the constraint:

> If a person who understands the meaning of sentences
> S and S' of language L can consistently accept S and
> not accept S', then S and S' must express different
> propositions.

Howard Wettstein argues that referentialist theories are clearly correct, but just as clearly cannot meet the constraint. He concludes that the constraint is a methodological mistake; that semantics *has* rested on a mistake (Wettstein, 1986, Wettstein, 1991). The job of the semanticist is to get the truth-conditions right, to provide a theory that tells us what propositions various sentences express. It is a mistake to suppose that this must provide us with a theory of cognitive significance.

In this book, I attempt to accept both Frege's cognitive constraint (or something recognizably descended from it) and the insights of referentialism. I cannot accept that a semantic theory can be correct that does not provide us with an appropriate interface between what sentences mean, and how we use them to communicate beliefs in order to motivate and explain action. A theory of linguistic meaning should provide us with an understanding of the properties sentences have that lead us to produce them under different circumstances, and react as we do to their utterance by others.

To accept the straightforward formulation above, however, would be to abandon hope for this reconciling project. That merely shows, I think, that this formulation is too strong. It builds in the assumption that the proposition expressed by an utterance is the only cognitively significant property that a semantics provides. I argue that this is not true, especially in the case of referentialist semantics. This formulation of the cognitive constraint allows a little more room for maneuver:

> If there is some aspect of meaning, by which an utterance u of S and an utterance u' of S' differ, so that a rational person who understood both S and S' might accept u but not u', then a fully adequate semantics should say what it is.

To see how a referentialist semantics might do this, let's return to the thread of our discussion and look at descriptivist theories of indexicals and demonstratives. It is one such theory that I think holds the key to resolving our dilemma.

1.4 The reflexive-referential theory

As in the case with names, the descriptivist position on indexicals and demonstratives comes in two basic varieties. One can hold that statements involving indexicals express propositions that incorporate identifying conditions that the speaker associates with the individual the indexical designates. Or one can hold that the identifying conditions derive from the rules of language. In the case of indexicals, it is the second position that has proven more attractive, in the form of the theory of token-reflexives. On this view, in more or less the form Reichenbach gave it, the proposition associated with (4) is a proposition about the token of 'I' in (4)—hence 'reflexive'; the proposition is about the token of 'I' *itself*. Call the token of 'I' in (4) 'ι'. Then the proposition associated with (4) is

(P^x4)   That *the speaker of* ι is a computer scientist.

(The superscript 'x' signals that this is a reflexive content; a superscript 'r' will signal referential content; the use of boldface and italic can be ignored for the moment; it will be explained in the next chapter.)

One can surely claim at least this, in favor of the token-reflexive theory: (P^x4) clearly is *one* thing that a competent speaker learns from an utterance of (4). To see this, imagine that when he says (4) David is not visible to the speaker. Perhaps an urgent call has gone out from a meeting for a computer scientist to resolve some particularly algorithmic problem, and David, as he rushes up the hall responding to the emergency, shouts (1) to reassure the waiting crowd. His token travels faster than he does, and reaches the meeting room before him. The crowd hears the token, grasps (P^x4), and is reassured, although though they don't yet know who the speaker is. The semantically competent members of the crowd will grasp (P^x4) simply in virtue of hearing the token and recognizing its type. (P^x4) is a proposition associated with (4) simply in virtue of the meaning of the type, 'I am a computer scientist'.

Reichenbach's theory is the starting point for the reflexive-referential theory I develop in this book. Oversimplifying a bit for introductory purposes, I'll call (P^x4) the *reflexive* content of (4). (Later I'll distinguish among various reflexive contents.) (P^x4) is reflexive because it is about the utterance (4) it*self*. Reflexive contents provide a solution to the co-reference and no-reference problems. Suppose that, after David makes it to the meeting room, a member of the crowd points at him and utters,

(6)   You are a computer scientist.

We can distinguish between the reflexive and referential contents of (6). Dub the token of 'you' in (6) τ. Then the reflexive content of (6) is

(P^x6)   That *the addressee of the speaker of* τ is a computer scientist.

while the referential content is,

(P^{r}6)   That **David Israel** is a computer scientist.

The referential content of (6) is the same as that of (4), but their reflexive contents differ. Even though the speaker of ι is the addressee of τ, (P^{x}4) is a quite different proposition than (P^{x}6); (P^{x}4) is about ι and (P^{x}6) is about τ, for one thing. At the level of reflexive content, the co-reference problem does not arise.

Suppose now that David does not arrive, and the group sits forlornly waiting for a computer scientist to rescue them. A noise is heard, which one member of the crowd takes to be a knock at the door. She utters (6) hopefully. But in this case, there is no addressee; no one is there; it was only ice falling on the stoop. So there is no referent for this utterance of 'you' in her utterance of (6), and no referential content. But that does not mean there is no reflexive content; it is still given by (P^{x}6).

Reichenbach's proposal, then, has merit. It provides, as contents for statements involving indexicals, propositions that are linked directly to utterances by meaning, that are clearly grasped by semantically competent listeners, and that avoid the co-reference and no-reference problems. But there are a number of objections to his proposal. In the first place, (P^{x}4) clearly is *not* what David *says* as he hurries down the hall. He is not talking about his own words but about himself. And (P^{x}6) clearly does *not* capture what the person in the meeting room says with (6), either in the case in which we imagine her talking to David, or in the case in which we imagine her talking to no one.

In the second place, reflexive contents would appear to provide a solution to the co-reference and no-reference problems only in the case of indexicals. Names are not indexicals. The referent of a name is not determined by some contextual feature of the situation of use, such as who is speaking or to whom or which objects are demonstrated. One can use a name to refer to anyone one can think of with that name; one does not need to know the physical relation of that person to the token, for it does not matter. It seems that the same phenomenon is at work with the co-reference and no-reference problems in the case of indexicals and names. Especially given the first objection, it seems unwise to adopt a solution to the problems for indexical cases that will not extend to cases involving names.

I shall argue, however, that these objections can be met. My argument rests on two basic ideas.

With respect to the first point, following an important paper by Arthur Burks, I shall argue that statements involving indexicals have two contents, which I call 'indexical' and 'referential'. The indexical contents are a species of reflexive contents; that is, they are propositions about the utterance itself. The referential contents are, at least in most cases, the 'official contents'; they are 'what is said' by the person making the statement. They are about the subject matter of the utterance, not the utterance itself. The counterfactual and same-saying arguments apply to referential contents. But referential contents alone do not suffice to provide us with an account of the cognitive significance of utterances. For that we need reflexive contents as well.

With respect to the second point, I make a distinction between indexicality, the special case, and reflexivity, the general case. Any statement, whether or not it contains indexicals, has multiple reflexive contents associated with it, which will be grasped by a semantically competent listener and are necessary for an account of cognitive significance. Suppose, for example, that you hear me utter (5),

(5)   David Israel is a computer scientist

but that you have no idea who David Israel is. You know, however, how proper names work. You know that my utterance will be true just in case (roughly) the following proposition is true:

(P^x5)   *The person named 'David Israel' to whom the use of it in* (5) *refers*, is a computer scientist

(P^x5) is certainly not the proposition expressed by (5). It is, however, a proposition that gives reflexive truth-conditions for (5), that a semantically competent speaker will grasp.

In this case the reflexivity does not derive from indexicality. Indexicality is simply a special case in which reflexivity is, so to speak, exploited by meaning. But, I shall argue, there are a wide variety of reflexive contents that we can and should appeal to in explaining the cognitive significance of language. And, I shall argue, if we examine carefully what the problems that cases of co-reference and no-reference pose for semantic theory, we shall see that these problems can be solved at the level of reflexive content.

The basic idea of the book, then, is that there are both reflexive and referential contents. The referentialist is right, basically, that 'what is said', the official contents of statements, are referential contents. There is some question of how rigidly this identity holds, whether the referential contents are always what is said, or only in what one might think of as the default case. But basically, the referentialist is right about what is said. The descriptivist is right, in holding that to explain the cognitive significance of statements we need to associate identifying conditions with the names and indexicals. These are found at the level of reflexive content.

1.5 Intentionality and network content

These tools handle the co-reference problem satisfactorily, or so I argue. Reflexive contents allow us to get at the multiplicity of ways we can think about and refer to the same object. But to handle the no-reference cases we need another layer of content, which I explain in terms of 'notion-networks' and call *intentional* content.

The term 'intentionality' is used by philosophers to get at phenomena connected with the 'object-directedness' of thought and language, and particular the phenomenon of object directedness where there is no object. Children all around the world are expecting Santa Claus to come on Christmas eve. Thoughtful readers around the world think that Sherlock Holmes was a better detective than the real Los Angeles detective Mark Furman.

Even though there is no Santa Claus, and no Sherlock Holmes, people can think about them, and think about them in different ways. While our reflexive contents allow us to explain multiple takes on the same object, they do not provide an account about shared beliefs about an object that doesn't exist.

The key here, I shall argue, is to consider what is involved in the flow of information and misinformation using language, and especially how the use of names and pronouns allows us to refer to objects that *do* exist. Our use of names and our talk about objects with which we are not interacting with depends on our participation in causal, historical, and informational chains of the sorts noted by Kaplan, Kripke, Donnellan, Evans and others. I call these 'notion-networks'. I can think of and talk about Aristotle because of a notion-network that has been going on since he was born. My use of 'Aristotle' is supported by this network. Aristotle is the origin of the network. My grandchild Anissa and her friends also participate in a network, one that stretches back to a series of nineteenth-century events that set up a network with no origin, and that supports the use of the term 'Santa Claus', by believers and non-believers alike.[2] To say Anissa and Everett expect the same person to come, or that Nathasha doesn't believe in the same person Anissa and Everett do believe in, is to say no more than that their beliefs, doubts, desires, and pretences are supported by the same network.

Once we recognize the importance of networks we can introduce a level of content, network content, that is in a sense between reflexive and official content. The network is a public object. It is these networks, I claim, that provide the structure that allows us to speak of beliefs that are directed at the same object, even when there is no object at which they are directed.

---

[2]This network co-opted one dating from the eighth century and Saint Nicholas, in the language I'll explain in chapter 7. See the article 'Santa Claus' in the 1987 *Encyclopedia Americana*.

1.6   Plan

After fixing some ideas and terminology in chapter 2, the first item of business will be to develop the reflexive-referential account of indexicals and demonstratives. This I do in chapter 3-5. In chapter 3, after discussing Burks' theory and its relation to the reflexive-referential theory, I discuss how indexicals work, semantically and cognitively. This requires a distinction between tokens and utterances, consideration of various types of contexts and contextual features that are relevant to various expressions.

In chapter 5 I discuss Reichenbach's idea, give an account of the meanings, reflexive contents and referential contents of statements containing indexicals and demonstratives, and apply these ideas to resolving the co-reference problem for demonstratives and indexicals. In chapter 6 I apply these ideas to proper names. This involves providing an account of how names work that allows us to apply the tools of reflexive content to them. I argue that reflexive content is the level relevant to cognitive significance, while referential content is official content, 'what is said'. Thus reflexive content is used to provide a solution to the co-reference problems, while subject matter content is what the referentialists arguments are about.

In chapters 7 and 8 I turn to the no-reference problem. I develop an account of notion-networks in chapter 7. In chapter 8 I fit pronouns into this account, and use it to discuss empty names and intentionality.

In chapter 9 I briefly return to the arguments for and against referentialism and descriptivism. First I discuss Frege's argument in the first paragraph of his essay 'Über Sinn und Bedeutung'. Then I turn to the question of whether the reflexive-referential theory can be used to defend what Ken Taylor calls 'the psychologized Fregean' in 'Meaning, Reference and Cognitive Significance' (1995); that is, whether the reflexive-referential theory can allow us to respect Frege's cogntive constraint while defending some version of referentialism. Finally I turn to Kaplan's arguments for direct reference in his *Demonstratives*. I argue that the reflexive-referential theory captures all of the valid insights of the arguments of Frege and Kaplan, while respecting a reasonable version of Frege's cognitive constraint.

2

Contents and Propositions

2.1 Introduction

The key concept in the debate between referential and descriptive approaches to the meaning of names and indexicals is that of content: *what is said* and *what is believed*. Referentialists rely on intuitions about content to make their case. Descriptivists complain that the referentialists' candidates for content cannot deal with the co-reference and no-reference problems. The innovation of the present treatment is to provide a family of contents, that meet the needs of both referentialists and descriptivists. In this chapter I make a few points about content, and explain my terminology. At the end of the chapter I develop an important distinction made by Genoveva Marti (1995), which helps to frame and clarify the debate between referentialism and descriptivism.

2.2 Meaning and content

A statement's *content* is a proposition that incorporates the conditions under which the statement is true. I use 'statements' to mean particular utterances, written or spoken, of declarative sentences. Statements are the kinds of utterances I will mainly discuss, so when I think of the success conditions of an utterance I'll have truth and falsity in mind. Contents belong to particular utterances, and should not be confused with *meanings*, which belong to *types* of expressions. Meanings are the rules that assign contents to the uses of expressions—that is, to particular utterances. They are among the rules we learn when we learn how to speak a language. 'Meaning' and 'content' are probably near synonyms in ordinary talk about language; I follow a fairly young tradition in using these terms to mark this important distinction. The contents of utterances of subsentential expressions reflect the contributions they make to truth-conditions of statements in which they occur.

For example, an utterance of sentence (4) by David Israel has the content that he is a computer scientist and is true, while an utterance of the same sentence by me, with the same meaning, has the content that I am a computer scientist, and is false. The sentence 'I am a computer scientist' has the same meaning in both cases, but by following the same rules we arrive at different truth conditions for them.

On a certain paradigm, important in the development of logic and many traditional concepts in the philosophy of language, expressions are supposed to be 'equisignificant'. (The term is Reichenbach's.) In our terms, an equisignificant expression is one the meaning of which fully settles the contents of utterances of it, the same for each of them. For equisignificant expressions, the meaning-content distinction is hardly worth making. The context of a particular utterance may be relevant to determining which expressions and which meanings are involved, but this is 'pre-semantic'. Once we have the meanings, the specifics of the utterance can be ignored.

Indexicals mess up this pretty picture. As I said, when Israel and I each utter sentence (4), the contents of our remarks are different, although the meanings of our sentences are the same. With indexicals, meaning stays the same, while the content can shift from utterance to utterance. To get things straight we need to be careful about the meaning-content distinction. We have to bring utterances and the relevant contextual factors into our semantics, as well as expressions. How this is done is the topic of chapters 3-5.

2.3 Common sense and official content

The concept of the content of a statement is a fairly robust concept of common sense. Our most basic idea of it is 'what is said' by a person who makes a statement; but I shall argue that this concept needs to be extended. By saying content is a is fairly robust concept, I mean that people with a bit of training and reflection make confident and fairly consistent judgements about it over a wide range of cases. For example, most people would say that it is not part of what David says, when he utters (4), that he is an English speaker, or that he is using the first person, or that he is speaking. And most people would agree that it is part of what David says that he is a computer scientist.

Our concept of what is said, of the content of a statement, is linked with other common sense concepts, such as the content of a belief—what is believed. We assume that if the speaker is sincere, semantically competent, and not confused, the content of the belief that motivates him to make a statement is simply the content of the statement itself. That is, we assume that what a sincere speaker says is what he believes. And of course there are a number of other 'propositional attitudes' that are linked to belief, other attitudes, and the use of language. We regularly infer the contents of people's 'propositional attitudes', their beliefs, desires, fears, hopes, and expectations, from the contents of their words; their words express their attitudes. If we consider the complexity of human brains and human lives, the extent to which we can anticipate, plan, predict and control human activity through the use of language is somewhat amazing. The propositional attitudes and the concept of content are powerful tools for dealing with very complex phenomena.

The core of our common-sense concept of content—*what* is said, *what* is believed—I will call *official content*. By and large I will take referentialist argument to be about official content, and agree with their conclusions about it. The other concepts of content I shall develop are not alternatives to official content, but systematic extensions of it that help to explain and locate it within a system. The basis for descriptive approaches and the solutions they pose for referentialist accounts are found in these other contents. All of these contents will be propositions that embody the truth-conditions associated with a particular statement in virtue of its meaning and context. What will vary will be which of those conditions of truth are taken as fixed and which are allowed to vary, in conceptualizing what a statement's truth requires.

2.4 The classificatory concept of content

A proposition is an abstract object. As such, it does not have any causal powers, at least not according to my way of looking at things. But the cognitive states we identify in terms of propositions do have causal powers. The false belief that Omaha is the capital of Nebraska, for example, might lead one to say something false when Regis asks, "What is the capital of Nebraska." It might cause one to drive to Omaha in order to see the famous capital building, and so forth. Grasping and believing that Lincoln is the capital of Nebraska is a different state, with different causal powers. Being in this state will dispose one to answer the question 'What is Nebraska's capital' correctly, and to drive towards Lincoln to see the famous building.

Some philosophers, notably Frege in 'The Thought' (1967a), seem to think of propositions not only as abstract objects, but as a very special kind of object, denizens of a Platonic 'third realm'. Fregean *Gendanken* seem to be intrinsically involved in cognitive states, and to determine the causal powers of those states, without having such powers themselves. Conversely, sometimes propositions are confused with internal representations, the complexes of ideas that many of our cognitive states involve.[3] My conception, in contrast, is that propositions are abstract objects we use to *classify* cognitive states, especially states that involve representations. Propositions are not representations, but abstract objects that we use to classify states and events by the requirements their truth (or some other form of success) impose on the

---

[3]See 'Propositional Attitudes' in Fodor, 1981.

rest of the world. Representations are not abstract objects, but concrete physical objects, states and events that have causes and effects.

Propositions are a bit analogous to weights and lengths, and the states that they classify are a bit analogous to the complex concrete physical factors that constitute an object's having the weight or length that it has. The fact that I weigh one hundred and ninety pounds explains why the scale moves as far as it does when I stand on it, why it takes several grandchildren to balance me on a teeter-totter. One hundred and ninety pounds is an abstract object, defined by its place in a system of such objects, which are systematically assigned to concrete objects and used to describe and predict the nature of events in which these concrete objects are involved. Mathematical relations among the system of weights correspond to empirical relations among the things classified by them. I am a very concrete object whose activities cause all sorts of things. If I am on one end of of a teeter-totter with one hundred and eighty five pounds of grandchildren on the other, then my end will go down. It is the causal powers of my body, bestowed on it by the mass of its parts, that makes it correctly classifiable as weighing one hundred and ninety pounds.

Similarly with my belief that Lincoln is the capital of Nebraska. I am in a cognitive state, that will cause me to say "Lincoln" when Regis asks what Nebraska's capital is, and to drive towards Lincoln if I want to see Nebraska's capital building. The proposition that correctly classifies this belief does so in virtue of the belief's causes and causal powers, its influence on the inferences I draw and the actions I perform.

The sort of content which I ascribe to utterances is intended to be naturalistic; it derives ultimately from the content of cognitive states, and the content of cognitive states derives ultimately from the *informational content of states and events* and *success conditions of acts*. I do not attempt to explain the relations between these concepts in this book, but I will briefly look at these two basic concepts to note some things about their structure that carries over to all kinds of naturalistic content.

The informational content of an event is *what the the world must be like in order for the event to have occurred*. Such content is relative to constraints or laws: they are the source of the 'must' in 'must be like'. There is a newspaper on my porch in the morning. Its being there carries the information that — 'shows that' or 'indicates that'—the newspaper-person delivered it. That must have happened — the world beyond the state of my porch here and now must contain such a prior event. It must, that is, given the way the world works: newspapers don't materialize out of nothing; they are not dropped from planes; the post office doesn't make early morning deliveries. They only appear on porches when people who are paid to deliver them there do so. Only relative to such constraints, laws, regularities, customs, etc. does the state of my porch contain information about what happened earlier in the day. And only if I have somehow internalized these constraints, so they guide my thinking, does the state of my porch lead me to believe in the earlier event. Only in this case does the circumstance of my porch *mean* anything to me about earlier events.

If I know or assume certain particular facts about the world, I may draw more particular inferences. If I know that the newspaper delivery person is Elwood Fritchey, then the paper being there will tell me *that Elwood has been there, that Elwood is awake and functioning*, and so forth. The informational content of an event or state, then, is relative to constraints and particular facts. If I think, "that shows *that someone delivered the newspaper*", I am classifying the state of my porch by what the rest of the world must be like for the newspaper to have gotten there *given* the way newspapers get delivered. If I think "that shows *that Elwood delivered the newspaper*", I am classifying the state of my porch by what the rest of the world must be like for the newspaper to have gotten there, given that constraint *and* the fact that Elwood is the delivery person. These are not alternative candidates for *the* informational content of the event, but two contents the event has, relative to different things taken as given.

The success-conditions of an act are relative not only to constraints but also to goals or chosen end-states. The success conditions of an act are what the world has to be like for the act to achieve the chosen end state. Suppose I try to swat a fly on the table. The action will succeed, relative to the goal of killing a fly, and given physics and some general facts or constraints about the ways flies and fly-swatters are constructed, if it is the case *that there is a fly in the path of the fly-swatter at the moment of its impact with the table*. That proposition is the success-condition of that act, relative to those constraints and that goal. Relative to the more soft-hearted goal of getting flies to move off the table without hurting them, the success condition for the very same movement would be different.

Suppose now that I have a certain fly that is my nemesis, which I have named Milton. I want not only to swat the fly on the table, I want to swat Milton. The two goals are compatible. I want to swat Milton *by* swatting the fly on the table. My intention has an *architecture* of goals, which generate different but systematically related and perfectly compatible success-conditions.

Intelligence derives from mechanisms that tend to trigger actions when their success-conditions are met. The informational content of the of the 'perception' that drives the act entails the success-conditions of the act. For example, the snapping of a mouse trap is successful when there is a mouse in the path of the blade. A well-designed mousetrap will release the blade when the platform that holds the cheese is disturbed, an event which indicates that a mouse is in front of the cheese platform, and hence in the path of the blade. The design of the mousetrap is intelligent relative to the goal of killing mice, and the constraint, among others, that only mice will disturb the cheese platform. I see a naturalistic approach to content as developing a variety of notions of content, including cognitive content and linguistic content, on the foundation of informational content and success conditions.[4]

---

[4]See Dretske, 1981; Barwise and Perry, 1983; Perry, 1990b; Israel and Perry, 1990; Israel and Perry, 1991; Stalnaker, 1984.

I don't propose to develop or defend these ideas in this book much beyond what I have just said. The point of saying this much is twofold. First, I want to reassure naturalists that the concept of *content* with which I am dealing is intended to be capable of naturalistic treatment. Second, I want to plant the suggestion that all sorts of naturalistic content, resting as they do on the pillars of informational content and success conditions, will be susceptible to classification by a *system of contents* and not simply a single content. The application of this idea to linguistic content is the central idea of his book.

Given this classificatory and naturalistic conception of the cognitive and linguistic attitudes, my account need not be wedded to any particular conception of propositions. A theory of propositions is a matter of constructing a system of abstract objects to classify contents, especially those of cognitive states and linguistic acts; there are a variety of ways of thinking of propositions that could suit our purposes satisfactorily. There are two main approaches to propositions in the literature today, the conception of a proposition as a set of possible worlds, and a number of conceptions of structured propositions—conceptions which pick up and develop a strand in Russell's thinking.[5] I think of propositions structurally. But I'll often consider the possible worlds in which a given proposition is or isn't true. The distinctions I need can be made in any number of more detailed approaches, and I don't need to develop an elaborate and formal ontology to say what I want. Moreover, given my focus on simple sentences, we only need that part of a theory that can allow us to make the distinctions needed to say what we want about the statements we make with such sentences.

2.5 Conditions and propositions

Consider:

(7)   Jim was born in Lincoln

---

[5]See Perry, 'Individuals in Informational and Intentional Content' (1990).

(7) is a statement of mine, in which names refer to my son Jim Perry and to Lincoln, Nebraska. On the referentialist view of proper names (7) expresses a *singular* proposition, a proposition that is about Jim himself and Lincoln itself, rather than any descriptions or attributes of them. This is what I called an 'R-proposition' in *The Problem of the Essential Indexical* (Perry, 2000). I'll designate this proposition in the following way:

(7P)   **Jim** was born in **Lincoln**.

The items in bold face are the *subject matter* of the statement and the *constituents* of the singular proposition. The truth of this proposition puts a condition on Jim himself, and Lincoln, itself. In some of the possible worlds in which this proposition is true Jim will not be named 'Jim'; in some he will look different than he in fact does, act differently than he in fact does, have a different job than he in fact has, and so forth. And in some of the worlds Lincoln may be named 'Davis' or 'McClellan'. In some of them Omaha or Nebraska City may be the capital of Nebraska rather than Lincoln. As long as Jim was born in Lincoln in a given world then the proposition is true in that world, whatever he is like and whatever he is called in that world, and whatever Lincoln is like and whatever it is called.

On the possible worlds conception of propositions, this proposition just *is* the set of worlds in which Jim was born in Lincoln.[6] On this conception the word 'constituent' is not strictly accurate, and if we stick to this conception exclusively, we have some problems in dealing with the intuitive concept of a proposition being about an object (Perry, 1986a). On a structural conception of propositions, one usually thinks of (7P) as some kind of set-theoretical object, say an ordered pair of a condition (*being born in*) and a sequence of objects (Jim and Lincoln), true if and only if the objects satisfy the condition. On such a structural conception, it is natural to say that Jim himself is a constituent of the proposition. As I said, I think of propositions as abstract objects,

---

[6]Or the function from worlds to truth-values that returns true for worlds in which Jim was born in Lincoln and false for the others.

perhaps sets or perhaps something specially developed for the purposes of philosophy and logic. Nothing in this book should turn on *which* conception. Moreover, although on this conception we don't identify the proposition with a set of worlds, we can still naturally talk about the worlds in which a proposition is true or false.

In fact, Jim is the manager of Kinko's[7], and Lincoln is the capital of Nebraska. Consider,

(8)   The manager of Kinko's was born in the capital of Nebraska.

On the standard account of definite descriptions, (8) expresses what Kaplan calls a *general* proposition, a proposition that is not specifically about Jim and Lincoln, but about being the manager of Kinko's, and being the capital of Nebraska. I'll designate this proposition as follows:

(P8)   That *the manager of Kinko's* was born in *the capital of Nebraska*

Here the boldface tells us which things we're thinking of as the subject matter. The italics tells us that is the identifying conditions *being the manager of Kinko's* and *being the capital of Nebraska* that are the subject matter, and not the objects they designate. If we wrote down the same thing but without the italics, we would not designate (P8). We would instead designate (P7), our singular proposition about Jim and Lincoln, in a new way:

(P7)   That **The manager of Kinko's** was born in **the capital of Nebraska**

(P8) is quite different than (P7). (P8) is true in worlds in which someone—it doesn't have to be Jim—is the manager of Kinko's and some city—it doesn't have to be Lincoln—is the capital of Nebraska, and the someone was born in the city. Consider the

---

[7] I use 'Kinko's' as a name for the Kinko's store on P street in Lincoln. Although Jim was manager of the Kinko's in Lincoln when this book was first drafted, as it nears completion he has moved to Kinko's headquarters in Ventura, California, where he is Manager of Technical Training.

possible world in which Jim is born in Grand Island, Omaha is the capital of Nebraska, and Marlon Brando (or Henry Fonda or Saul Kripke or some other native Omahan)[8] manages the Kinko's in Lincoln. In these worlds (P8) would be true, but (P7) would be false.

Instead of italics, we could use David Kaplan's indexical 'dthat(ψ)' to get at the difference between (P7) and (P8). 'The manager of Kinko's' would give us the identifying condition, while 'dthat(the manager of Kinko's) would give us Jim. So we would have:

(P7)   That dthat(the manager of Kinko's) was born in dthat(the capital of Nebraska).

(P8)   That *the manager of Kinko's* was born in *the capital of Nebraska*.

The use of italics and boldface will be convenient for our purposes, because it allows us to use something very close to ordinary English as our language for talking about propositions. The cost of convenience is a bit of possibly misleading ambiguity. Jim was born in Lincoln, and dthat(the manager of Kinko's) was born in dthat(the capital of Nebraska), and it is true that *the manager of Kinko's* was born in *the capital of Nebraska*. But identifying conditions are not the kinds of things that get born, or that things get born in. The relation of *being born in* does not hold between the identifying condition *being the manager of Kinko's* and *being the capital of Nebraska*. What (8) tells us, and (P8) is intended to capture, is that the relation of *someone who fits the first was born in some place that fits the second* holds between the two identifying conditions. We may have to occasionally remind ourselves of this ambiguity, but for the most part handling it comes natural to natural language speakers, and it won't cause problems.

I'll say that (P7) is the result of *loading* (P8) with the facts that Jim is the manager of Kinko's, and Lincoln is the capital of

---

[8] Actually, I'm not sure these famous people who grew up in Omaha were all born there.

Nebraska. Or, a bit more precisely, (P7) is the result of loading the first identifying condition in (P8) with the fact that Jim is manager of Kinko's and the second identifying condition of (P8) with the fact that Lincoln is the capital of Nebraska.

Now consider,

(9)   Jim was born in the capital of Nebraska.

(P9)   That **Jim** was born in *the capital of Nebraska*.

(10)   The manager of Kinko's was born in Lincoln.

(P10)   That *The manager of Kinko's* was born in **Lincoln**.

Statement (9) expresses (P9), the proposition that results from loading only the first identifying condition of (P8).[9] Statement (10) expresses (P10), the proposition that results from loading only the second identifying condition of (P8).

As (9) and (10) illustrate, the distinction between singular and general propositions is a bit too simple. (9) would ordinarily be taken to express a singular proposition; *being singular* is sort of a dominant characteristic, so that if at least one argument role of a condition is filled by an object, the result is singular even if the other argument roles are filled by identifying conditions. I will speak this way, but we have to keep in mind that the basic concept is that of an argument role being filled either by an object or by an identifying condition of an object—the singular/general dichotomy is just a useful oversimplification.

We also need to think about conditions as having individuals or identifying conditions as constituents. Consider, these two conditions, the first from (9), the second from (10).

(C9)   That x was born in *the capital of Nebraska*.

(C10)   That x was born in **Lincoln**.

---

[9]We also allow that an identifying condition can be loaded by a mere state of affairs—a would-be fact.

(C9) is a general condition, with the identifying condition, *the capital of Nebraska* as a constituent, while (C10) is a singular condition, because it has the city, Lincoln, as a constituent.

Now let's go back and look again at (8).

(8)   The manager of Kinko's was born in the capital of Nebraska.

As we saw, (8) expresses (P8), in which both argument roles of the condition *x was born in y* are filled by identifying conditions.

(P8)   That *the manager of Kinko's* was born in *the capital of Nebraska*

But these identifying conditions themselves are singular, involving Kinko's and Nebraska as constituents, respectively. The worlds in which (P8) is true might differ as to who managed the Kinko's in Lincoln. Jim doesn't even have to in a world for (P8) to be true in it. But the Kinko's in Lincoln has to be there, because it is a constituent of the condition that someone must meet for (P8) to be true. And (P8) is true in worlds in which Lincoln doesn't exist, and the barren spot next to a salty creek where it was founded remains just that (except for the Kinko's). But Nebraska has to be in these worlds, as a constituent of the condition some city has to meet, for (P8) to be true.

Borrowing another of Kaplan's terms, I'll say that a proposition or condition is *purely qualitative* if as one goes down through the hierarchy of conditions involved in it, one never encounters an object, only more conditions. I'll call it *lumpy* if one encounters an object. The proposition expressed by (8), though general, is lumpy. I call the constituents of the identifying conditions of a proposition *covert* constituents of the proposition. Sometimes I'll get careless and call a proposition 'singular' when I should call it 'general but lumpy.'

This isn't much of a theory of propositions, but I think it will suffice for our purposes.

2.6 Varieties of designation

Consider once again:

(8)   The manager of Kinko's was born in the capital of Nebraska.

(9)   Jim was born in the capital of Nebraska.

By 'singular term', I mean to include definite descriptions as well as pronouns and proper names. I use 'designate' as a general word for the relation between singular terms and the objects they stand for. Thus the subject terms of both (7) and (8) *designate* the same person, Jim Perry.

Within the category of designating singular terms, we need to make two pairs of distinctions.[10]

Denoting versus naming. The first distinction has to do with the 'mechanisms' of designation. I'll say that a term *denotes* if the conventions of language associated it with an identifying condition, and the term designates whatever object meets that condition. I'll say that a term *names* if the conventions of languages associate it with the object(s) it designates.

Definite descriptions are the paradigm denoting terms. Language associates definite descriptions with identifying conditions. Definite descriptions are only indirectly associated with the objects they designate, as the objects that fit the identifying condition associated by meaning. So, in virtue of its meaning, 'The manager of Kinko's ' is associated with a certain identifying condition. It designates Jim Perry not simply in virtue of its meaning, but in virtue of its meaning and his job.

With names things are more controversial. A number of philosophers have maintained that names denote; they are 'hidden' descriptions. On this issue, however, referentialist argu-

---

[10]Genoveva Marti presents these distinctions (using somewhat different terminology) forcefully in 'The Essence of Genuine Reference'. On this topic and elsewhere I also owe a great debt to Francois Recanati's *Direct Reference* (1993), a work that can be profitably consulted on virtually any topic connected with indexicality and reference.

ments have proven persuasive. The standard view, and the view I maintain in this essay, is that names name. The convention I invoke, when I use 'Jim' to refer to my oldest son, is not a convention that associates the name with a condition which, as it happens, he fulfills. It's just a convention that says that 'Jim' is his name—a convention established when he was born and that name was used on his birth certificate.

It is easy to be led astray here. Suppose you see Jim at a party, and ask me what his name is. I tell you, and thus disclose to you a certain naming convention. Now you will be thinking of Jim Perry in a certain way at that point, perhaps as 'the man I am looking at and just asked the name of and heard saying something interesting about computers a minute ago'. So, when I tell you that man's name is 'Jim', the link in your mind may be between the name and a certain identifying condition of him. This does not mean that the *convention* I have disclosed to you is a convention linking the name with that identifying condition or any other. The convention links the name with Jim; it has been around since he was born, and so long before he had anything interesting to say about computers; the identifying condition is relevant only because that is how you happen to be thinking of him.

There are then two quite different forms an answer to the question 'Why does term t designate object a', may take. If t denotes, the answer will have two parts:

> (i) The meaning of t assigns identifying condition C to t;

and

> (ii) a is the object that satisfies C.

If t names, the answer will just have one part:

> The meaning of t assigns a to t.

Describing versus referring Our second distinction has to do with the contribution terms make to the propositional content of a statement, what is said, what I'm calling 'official content'.

On standard accounts, the propositional contents of (7) and

(8) are different. (P7) is a singular proposition about Jim, while (P8) is a general proposition about being the manager of Kinko's. As we saw above, these are different propositions, true in different possible worlds. I use 'refers' and 'describes' to mark this distinction. These terms pertains to the contribution a term makes to the official propositional content of statements of which it is a part, and not to the mechanism of designation. The standard referentialist view of names, and the one I shall defend, is that they *refer*; that is, they contribute to (official) propositional content the individual they designate.

Almost everyone agrees that at least some of the time, definite descriptions *describe*; that is, they contribute to official content the identifying condition their meaning associates with them.[11] Keith Donnellan's famous distinction between referential and attributive uses of definite descriptions could be interpreted as the claim that definite descriptions do sometimes refer. However, I will supply a somewhat different account below.

Referentialism, with respect to a category of terms, is the thesis that those terms *refer*. It is a position about the contribution a term makes to official propositional content, not about the mechanism of reference. I will argue that names name and refer, and indexicals denote and refer. Thus I will be advocating referentialism. The account I develop, however, will be a moderate and benign form of referentialism that can handle problems of cognitive significance and intentionality, or so I shall argue.

---

[11]More accurately, in terms introduced below, definite descriptions contribute the condition associated with them by meaning and context, their content$_C$.

3

Utterance and Context

3.1 Introduction

When you use the word 'I' it designates you; when I use the same word, it designates me. If you use 'you' talking to me, it designates me; when I use it talking to you, it designates you. 'I' and 'you' are *indexicals*. The designation of an indexical *shifts* from speaker to speaker, time to time, place to place. Different utterances of the same indexical designate different things, because what is designated depends not only on the meaning associated with the expression, but also on facts about the utterance. An utterance of 'I' designates the person who utters it; an utterance of 'you' designates the person to whom it is addressed, an utterance of 'here' designates the place at which the utterance is made, and so forth. Because indexicals shift their designation in this way, sentences containing indexicals can be used to say different things on different occasions. Suppose you say to me, "You are wrong and I am right about reference," and I reply with the same sentence. We have used the same sentence, with the same meaning, but said quite different and incompatible things.

In addition to ' I' and 'you', the standard list of indexicals includes the personal pronouns 'my', 'he', 'his', 'she', 'it', the demonstrative pronouns 'that' and 'this', the adverbs 'here', 'now', 'today', 'yesterday' and 'tomorrow' and the adjectives 'actual' and 'present'. This list is from David Kaplan's 'Demonstratives' (1989); Kaplan's work on the semantics and logic of indexicals is responsible for much of the increased attention given to indexicals by philosophers of language in recent years. The words and aspects of words that indicate tense are also indexicals. And many other words, like 'local', seem to have an indexical element.

Philosophers have found indexicals interesting for at least two reasons. First, such words as 'I' and 'now' and 'this' play crucial roles in arguments and paradoxes about such philosophically rich subjects as consciousness, the self, the nature of time, and the nature of perception. Second, although the meaning of these words seems relatively straightforward, it has not been so obvious how to incorporate these meanings into semantical theory. I will focus on the second issue in this essay and, even with respect to that issue, discuss only a few of the many topics that deserve attention. Among other things, I won't consider tense, or plurals[12] quasi-indication[13] I'll focus on the words Kaplan listed, and among those on singular terms.

3.2 The reflexive-referential theory

In his pioneering work Arthur Burks (1949), distinguishes the following aspects of an utterance containing indexicals:

(i)   The sign itself, which is a token that occurs at a spatiotemporal location and which belongs to a certain linguistic type.

(ii)   The existential relations of the token to other objects.

(iii)   The meaning associated with the type.

(iv)   The indexical meaning of the token, which, in the case of tokens involving indexicals, goes beyond the type meaning.[14]

(v)   The information conveyed by the sign.

---

[12]See Nunberg, 1992, Nunberg, 1993, Vallee, 1996.

[13]See Castañeda, 1967, Corazza, 1995.

[14]Burks also uses the term 'symbolic meaning' for a property of tokens determined by the meaning of their type.

Suppose, for example, Burks tells me, pointing to a house on Monroe Street in Ann Arbor: "I live in that house." (i) The sign itself is the token or burst of sound that Burks utters; it is a token of an English sentence of a certain type, namely, 'I live in that house', and it occurs at a certain spatio-temporal location. (ii) This token has 'existential relations' to other objects. That is, *there is* a person who uttered it (Burks), *there is* a house at which that person was pointing at the time of utterance, and so forth. (iii) English associates a meaning with the type, the same for every token of it. Roughly, a token of 'I live in that house', will be true if the speaker of that token lives in the house he or she points to at the time they produce the token. This is what all tokens of the type have in common. (iv) Each token also has an *indexical meaning*, which results from the combination of the type meaning and the the particular token. Call the token Burks produced t. Imagine David Kaplan pointing to a house in Pacific Palisades at some other time and producing a token t' of the same sentence, 'I live in that house.' The tokens t and t' have the same type meaning, but different indexical meanings: t will be true if there is a house the speaker of t points at and he lives in it, t' will be true if there is a house the speaker of t' points at and he lives in it.

Aspect (v) is the information conveyed by the sign. Let's add a third token to our example. Let t″ be my token of 'You live in that house', said to Burks, pointing to the house on Monroe Street. My token doesn't have the same type or the same indexical meaning as t, Burks's token of 'I live in that house'. But there is something important that my token and Burks's token have in common. Each of them will be true if a certain person, Burks, lives in a certain house, the one on Monroe Street. Once we factor in the contextual or 'existential' facts that are relevant to each token, they have the same truth-conditions. Their truth places the same conditions on the same objects. Burks calls this 'conveying the same information'.

The reflexive-referential theory builds on Burks's basic framework. In this chapter and the next two, I go through the five aspects, often starting with a discussion of Burks's basic idea. I discuss various issues, elaborating and qualifying the basic idea; the reflexive-referential of indexicals theory is the account that emerges from this process. Here is an overview, highlighting the differences in terminology:

Aspect (i): Burks takes the sign itself to be the token. I think there is an ambiguity in 'token'; it is sometimes used for an act, a use of language, an instance of speaking, writing or signing. At other times 'token' is used for something produced by or at least used in such acts. I'll use 'utterance' for the first and reserve 'token' for the second. In some kinds of discourse tokens are epistemically basic, but utterances are always semantically basic. (As I use the word 'uttering' it includes writing as well as speaking.) I discuss these issues in the next section.

Aspect (ii): What Burks calls the 'existential relations' are now usually referred to as the 'context'; indexicals are expressions whose designation *shifts* from context to context. I will distinguish several different uses we make of context, and distinguish various contextual factors that are relevant to different types of indexicals. I discuss these issues in section the last section of this chapter and in chapter 4.

Aspect (iii): For Burks the 'type meaning' is associated by language with expressions. I simply call this 'meaning'—I try to always use 'meaning' for what the conventions of language associate with types. The key idea here in our account of the meaning of indexicals comes from Reichenbach, who emphasized the *reflexivity* of indexicals. I discuss these issues in chapter 5.

Aspects (iv) and (v): I take content to be a property of specific utterances. Burks recognizes two kinds of content, while I recognize three. What Burks calls 'indexical meaning' I call ' indexical content'. What Burks calls 'information conveyed' I call 'designational content'. I claim that neither of these is our official, intuitive notion of content; that is, neither corresponds to 'what is said' by an utterance. That role is played by 'referential content'. All three kinds of content, however, play important roles in the epistemology of language. I discuss these three kinds of content in chapter 5.

3.3 Signs, tokens and utterances

For Burks, the sign itself is simply the token. But the term 'token' is used in two ways in the literature. Sometimes it is used for the *act* of speaking, writing, or otherwise using language. At other times, it is used for an object that is produced by, or at least used in, such an act. Reichenbach, for example, introduces tokens as acts of speaking, but then a few pages later talks about the position of a token on a page, clearly thinking of the ink marks.

Some authors use 'tokening' for the first sense, but I shall use 'utterance'. Utterances are intentional acts. The term 'utterance' often connotes spoken language, but as I use it an utterance may involve speech, writing, typing, gestures or any other sort of linguistic activity.

I use 'token' in the second sense, in the way Reichenbach used it when he said that a certain token was to be found on a certain page of a certain copy of a book. In this sense, tokens are traces left by utterances. They can be perceived when the utterances cannot, and be can used as evidence for them. Modern technology allows for their reproduction. The paradigm tokens are the ink marks produced in writing or typing. When we read, tokens are epistemically basic, and the utterances that produced them hardly thought of. But the utterances are semantically basic; it is from the intentional acts of speakers and writers that the content derives.

An utterance may involve a token, but not be the act of producing it. My wife Frenchie and I were once Resident Fellows in a dormitory at Stanford, eating with the students each evening in the cafeteria. If she went to dinner before I returned from a late class, she would write on a small blackboard on the counter, "I have gone to the cafeteria," and set it on the table near the front door of our apartment. I would put it back on the counter. There was no need for her to write out the message anew each time I was late; if the blackboard had not been used for something else in the interim, she could simply move it from the counter back to the table. Frenchie used the same token to say different things on different days. Each use of the token was a separate utterance.

One can imagine the same token being reused as a token of a different type of sentence. Suppose there is a sign in a flying school, intended to warn would-be pilots: "Flying planes can be dangerous." The flying school goes bankrupt; the manager of a park near the airport buys the sign and puts it next to another sign that prohibits walking on high tightropes. In its new use the sign is a token of a type with a different syntax and a different meaning than in its original use. In principle, tokens could even be re-used for utterances in different languages; I leave finding such examples as an exercise for the reader.

In the case of spoken utterances in face to face communication, the utterance/token distinction becomes pretty subtle. One who hears the token will see the utterance which produces it. (In the case of signed utterances, as in American Sign Language, the distinction is subtler still.) Writing brings with it the possibility of larger gaps between use and perception; letters are sent, books are put on shelves, to be read months or even years later, and so forth. The utterance/token distinction is most at home in the case of written text. It grows in importance as culture and technology develop. The tokens we perceive in books are not ink marks directly produced by the author. Modern technology allows for the storage and reproduction of both spoken and written tokens, and with such devices as email, even a casual utterance may involve the production of numbers of tokens around the world.[15]

So, to review some distinctions and terminological decisions made thus far:

> *Tokens* are physical events or objects, bursts of sound or patterns of ink on page or pixels on a screen, that

---

[15]In 'Types, Tokens and Templates' (1992), David Levy and Ken Olson argue that to develop an account of documents adequate for the age of duplicating machines and computers we need to distinguish types, tokens and *templates*.

are used by agents in their utterances. They are typically produced by speaking, writing, typing, etc., and through devices for the reproduction and transmission of tokens. Tokens are perceived by listeners and readers, often providing the main evidence for the existence of and nature utterances.

An *utterance* is an act that involves the use of a token and typically the production of a new token. Utterances can be acts of speaking, writing, typing, signing, etc.

A *statement* is an utterance of a declarative sentence.

An *expression* is a type, either a word or a longer phrase such as a sentence. Types characterize both utterances and tokens.

The utterances of expressions that are parts of utterances of larger expressions are *subutterances*; e.g. an utterance of 'I was born in Lincoln' involves a subutterance of 'I'.

3.4   Context

What Burks calls the 'existential relations' of a token or utterance is now usually referred to as its 'context'. The 'context-dependence' of indexicals is often taken as their defining feature: what an indexical designates *shifts* from context to context. But there are many kinds of shiftiness, with corresponding conceptions of context. Until we clarify what we mean by 'context', this defining feature remains unclear.

Sometimes we use context to figure out with which meaning a word is being used, or which of several words that look or sound alike is being used, or even which language is being spoken. These are *presemantic* uses of context: context helps us to figure out meaning. In the case of indexicals, however, context is used *semantically*. It remains relevant after the language, words and meanings are all known; the meaning directs us to certain aspects of context. Both these uses of context differ from a third. In the third type of case we lack the materials we need for the proposition expressed by a statement, even though we have identified the words and their meanings, and have consulted the contextual factors the indexical meanings direct us to. Some of the constituents of the proposition expressed are *unarticulated*, and we consult the context to figure out what they are. I call this the 'content-supplementing' use of context. Finally and importantly we use context to interpret the intention with which the utterance was made; what was the speaker trying to do? This is the *pragmatic* use of context. In a sense, the main goal of this book is to provide pragmatics with a rich interface to semantics; still, I'll have little to say about pragmatics *per se*.

Presemantic uses of context

Consider this utterance:

(11)   Ich! (said by several teenagers at camp in response to the question, 'Who would like some sauerkraut').

Knowing that this happened in Berlin rather than San Francisco might help us determine that it was German teenagers expressing enthusiasm and not American teenagers expressing disgust. In this case context is relevant to figuring out which language (and hence which word with which meaning) is being used.

The vocable 'ich' is a *homonym* across languages. Homonyms are words that are spelled and pronounced alike. For example, there are two words in English that are spelled and pronounced 'quail'; one is a noun that stands for a small game bird, the other a verb for faltering or recoiling in terror. It makes sense to speak of two words that are pronounced and spelled the same, because words are not merely patterns of sound or combinations of letters, but cultural objects with histories; our two words 'quail' derived from different French and Latin words. The term 'vocable' can be used for what the words have in common, so if we need to be precise we can say the vocable 'quail' corresponds to two words in English.

Each of the German teen-agers, when they use the indexical 'ich', designates herself or himself, and so the expression 'ich' designates differently for each of them. One might be tempted to consider this just more homonymy. Each has a different name for himself or herself, they just happen to all be spelled alike and sound alike; we have homonyms across idiolects of the same language. Such a temptation should surely be resisted as an explanation of the shiftiness of indexicals. For one thing, the word 'ich' doesn't have different historical origins depending on which teen-ager uses it; they all learned the standard first-person in German. The homonym account would be even worse for temporal and spatial indexicals. We would have to suppose that I use a different word 'tomorrow' each day, since my use of 'tomorrow' shifts its designation every night at the stroke of midnight.

With both homonyms and indexicals we use context to help determine what is designated. In the case of homonyms, the context is anything about the facts surrounding the utterance that will help us to figure out which words are used. But in the case of 'I' or 'ich', we consult context after we know which expression we have, looking for a very specific fact—who the speaker is—to determine which object is designated in accordance with the meaning of that expression.

An *ambiguous* expression like 'bank' may designate one kind of thing when you say "Where's a good bank?" while worried about finances, another when I use it, thinking about fishing. Its designation varies with different uses, because different of its meanings are relevant. Again, all sorts of contextual facts may be relevant to helping us determine this. Is the speaker holding a wad of money or a fishing pole?

It isn't always simply the meaning of a particular word that is in question, and sometimes questions of meaning, syntax and the identity of the words go together:

(12)   I forgot how good beer tastes [16]

---

[16]Thanks to Ivan Sag for the examples.

(13)   I saw her duck under the table.

With (12), knowing whether our speaker has just arrived from Germany or just arrived from Saudi Arabia might help us to decide what the syntactic structure of the sentence is and whether 'good' was being used as an adjective or an adverb.

Is 'duck' a noun or a verb in (13)? In this case, knowing a little about the situation that this utterance is describing will help us to decide whether the person in question had lost her pet or was seeking security in an earthquake.

In each of these cases, the context, the environment of the utterance, the larger situation in which it occurs, helps us to determine what is said. But these cases differ from indexicals. In these cases it is a sort of accident, external to the utterance, that context is needed. We need the context to identify which name, syntactic structure or meaning is used because the very same shapes and sounds happen to be shared by other words, structures, or meanings. The appeal to context comes in determining the meaning. Thus these appeals to context are presemantic.

3.5   Semantic uses of context

In the case of indexicals we still need context *after* we determine which words, syntactic structures and meanings are being used. The meanings *exploit* the context to perform their function. The meaning of the indexical 'directs us' to certain features of the context, in order to fix the designation. A defining feature of indexicals is that the meanings of these words fix the designation of specific utterances of them in terms of facts about those specific utterances. The facts that meaning of a particular indexical deems relevant are the contextual facts for particular uses of it.

The third person pronouns, 'he', 'she' and 'it', the demonstrative pronouns 'this' and 'that' and demonstrative adjective phrases like 'this computer' and 'that man' can be used either deictically or for anaphoric co-designation. In either case, the role the designated object plays is less tightly bound to meaning than in the case of the classic indexical pronouns 'I' and 'you'.

In anaphoric co-designation what one word designates depends on what another word in the same bit of discourse, to which the word in question is anaphorically related, designates. Consider

(14)   Harold went into the Navy. He didn't like it.

(15)   Percy went into the Army. He didn't like it.

In (14) 'he' stands for Harold and 'it' stands for the Navy; in (15), these words stand for Percy and the Army. The designata depend on what the antecedents of 'he' and 'it' are, and what those antecedents stand for. But in the case in which you tell me "You are wrong about reference, and I am right," the designation of your uses of 'you' and 'I' do not depend on other words, but simply on the fact that you are speaking to me.

In both cases, the referent of the expression is the object that plays a certain *role* relative to the utterance. The use of the word, together with contextual facts, *directs* us to a certain object that plays this role. In the case of indexicals, the role takes us directly outside of language. 'I' refers to the speaker; a demonstrative use of 'that man' refers to the man the speaker indicates. In the case of anaphoric co-designation, the role is mediated by another bit of language. In (15) there are two 'conversational threads' made available by the first sentence. In the second he' picks up the first thread, 'it' the second. 'He' stands for Percy because its antecedent, 'Percy' does.

In the case of anaphoric co-designation, the contextual facts have to do with the relation of the utterance to previous noun-phrases in the discourse. In the case of indexicals and deictic uses, rather different sorts of facts are relevant, having to do with the relation of the utterance to things other than words, such as the speaker, addressee, time and place of the utterance. Consider, for example 'That man came to see me yesterday. He is interested in philosophy.' Resolving the reference of 'he' involves knowing two sorts of facts. First, one must know that the use of 'he' is anaphorically related to 'that man'. Second, one must know at which man the utterance context of 'that man' was directed.

Consider:

(16)   Some woman wrote a very interesting dissertation at UCLA and she advocated subjective semantics in it.

(17   Adele wrote a very interesting dissertation at UCLA. She advocated subjective semantics in it.

(18)   (Indicating a certain woman) She advocated subjective semantics in her UCLA dissertation.

How should we treat the occurrences of 'she' in (16), (17) and (18)? In (16) it seems be be a variable bound by 'Some woman'; in (17) a pronoun anaphorically connected to 'Adele'; in (18) a demonstrative pronoun. No one supposes these uses of 'she' are mere homonyms. Many philosophers are at least tempted to suppose they are occurrences of a single ambiguous word, which sometimes functions as a variable and sometimes as an indexical (Kaplan, 1989a). Most linguists find this implausible, and would prefer an account that gives a uniform treatment of pronouns.

Following Heim and Kratzer (1998) I see the cases of deictic or demonstrative uses of pronouns closely related to anaphoric co-designative uses, with the concept of salience at the core. Pronouns also have anaphoric connections with quantifier phrases, as in (16), and I am convinced there should be a unified treatment. However, I won't provide one in this book, but stick to the project of trying to deal with simple sentences.

3.6   Content-supplemental uses of context

Compare the following pairs of sentences:

(18a)   It is raining

(18b)   It is raining here

(19a)   They are serving drinks at the local bar

(19b)   They are serving drinks at the bar in this neighborhood.

In many circumstances (18a) and (18b) would convey exactly the same information, that it was raining where the speaker was. In both cases, the place where the rain must be taking place for the statement to be true is supplied by the context. But there is an important difference in how this place is supplied. In (18b) there is a part of the sentence, the indexical 'here', that designates the place. The relevant contextual fact is simply the place of the utterance. In (18a) there is no item in the sentence that designates the place. The contextual fact that provides the place is simply that it is obvious to everyone that the speaker is talking about the weather in the place she is at.

Suppose the speaker is talking on the phone with a relative who lives a number of miles away, where there has been a drought. She interrupts the conversation to utter (18a) to her family, gathered near the phone. In this case the reference is to the place where the relative is, not to the place where the speaker is. It is simply the facts about the speaker's intentions, perhaps limited by what the speaker can expect the audience to figure out, that determines which place is being talked about when (18a) is used.

In this case, I say that the place is an *unarticulated constituent* of the proposition expressed by the utterance. It is a constituent, because, since rain occurs at a time in a place, there is no truth-evaluable proposition unless a place is supplied. It is unarticulated, because there is no morpheme that designates that place.

I call these uses 'content-supplemental' because we look to context after we have all of the words and their meanings identified. Elsewhere I called this use of context 'postsemantic'. It is postsemantic if we think of 'semantic' as having to do with 'meaning'. If we think of semantics as determining *content*, 'postsemantic' is not a very good term. When we have the syntax of 'It is raining' and the meanings of each or the component words, we still don't have the content.

In the case of a sentence with an indexical in it, like 'It is raining here', the last step in determining content is a step from the meaning of 'here' to its content, the place of the utterance. In the case of 'It is raining' the last step is a step from a parametric content, the condition of raining at the present time, to the proposition that it is raining at a certain place. A more accurate but somewhat cumbersome phrase would be 'post-meaning but pre-content uses of context'.

The words 'local' in (19a) and 'near' in (19b) both identify a relation between objects (like bars) and locations. They differ syntactically, in that 'local' has one explicit argument place, for the bar, while 'near' has two, one for the bar and one for the location. But a location is needed with 'local' too; to determine whether (19a) is true or not, we need to determine not only which bars are serving drinks, but relative to which location the crucial bar is local. In many cases it will be the location where the speaker is, but it need not be. As a continuation of the aside mentioned above, (19a) could be a remark about the location where the relative on the other end of the phone call of (18a) finds himself, deciding whether to go home in the rain, or to stay dry and have a drink.

There is an unarticulated constituent of the condition 'local' as it occurs in (19a). Bars are local relative to neighborhoods; there is no morpheme in the phrase 'local' that refers to the neighborhood relative to which the bar has to be local. However, in the condition 'in this neighborhood' the neighborhood is articulated; it is the referent of 'this neighborhood'.

In thinking about unarticulated constituents and content - supplemental uses of context, we need to keep three possibilities in mind:

> A constituent is not articulated, and it is not easy to articulate it in the language in question without appeal to some general purpose phrase like 'according to' or 'relative to'. To articulate marks one as an innovator, or a philosopher, some kind of pedant, or perhaps someone with an agenda. For example you say, "The 49ers were unsuccessful last year," and I reply, "Yes, relative to the

standard measure of success." I agree that they were unsuccessful by the usual standards of success for professional football teams, winning, but maintain that they were successful, last year, relative to the standards of encouraging good sportsmanship, not having any players, coaches or owners indicted, and wearing tasteful uniforms.

A constituent is not articulated, and there is nothing explicit in the syntax that calls for it, but it is easy to articulate it. This is the case of (18a) and (18b). We all know that rain occurs at a place. There is nothing insightful or innovative about articulating it. But there is nothing syntactically incomplete about (18a).

A constituent is not articulated, leaving the sentence a bit odd, although the proposition conveyed is clear enough. You ask me, "Did the 49ers beat Philadelphia today?" I reply, "Philadelphia beat." My reply is not grammatical, but would still convey that Eagles beat the 49ers, just as the grammatical 'Philadelphia won' would.

In each of these cases we have what I call an unarticulated constituent; that is, a constituent of the proposition that is not the referent of some morpheme in the statement. On the way I like to look at things, relations have *argument roles* or parameters. These are to be distinguished from the *argument places* or *variables* that predicates that express the relations may have. My picture of unarticulated constituents is that there are argument roles that are not represented by explicit argument places. We fill the *argument role* which is filled from context. In the first case it is the standards of success; in the second case it is the place of the rain; in the third it is the team Philadelphia beat. In the third case, but not in the first, there is an argument place required by the grammar: 'Beat' is a transitive verb and requires a subject for the victor, and an object for the vanquished. But there is nothing ungrammatical 'Philadelphia won'. The metaphysics of winning requires a victor and a vanquished, but the grammar of 'won' does not require we identify the vanquished.

What about the middle case? There is a debate about whether in such cases the 'logical form' of a sentence like (18a) contains an argument place for the place, or does not. Francois Recanati and Jason Stanley have commandeered the term 'unarticulated constituent' for the purposes of this debate (Stanley, 2000). Stanley claims that there is such an argument place in logical form, hence the constituent is articulated; Recanati claims that there is no such place, hence it is not. I think it is a bad idea to use the term 'unarticulated constituent' for two different questions, and of course I like my use of it better.

On the issue in question, I am inclined to side with Recanati, I think. I conceive things in the following way. Relations are ways of classifying variations and unknowns across phenomena, against a background of factors that are taken as unchanging or otherwise given. The words for relations will be lexicalized in a way that reflects what is taken as varying and unknown, at least in a typical case, or was at the time the words acquired their grammatical properties. So 'be simultaneous' has two argument places for events, and none for inertial frames. 'Rain' has tense, but no argument place for places. 'Be successful' has tense and an argument place for succeeder, but none for the standards of success. We use adverbial and prepositional phrases of various sorts to get at additional relevant factors when we need to. In cases where this happens a lot, it will be easy. There are a lot of ways to say where it is raining. In cases in which scientific or philosophical discoveries or insights leads to appreciation of unlexicalized factors, we appeal to phrases like 'relative to'. So event are simultaneous *relative to* inertial frames; the 49ers were unsuccessful last year *relative to* the common standards of success for athletic teams.

There is an intuitive distinction between what someone literally said or asked and what is conveyed when we take into account why she said it or asked it. Traditionally, the first is included in semantics, the second in pragmatics.

If we are eating breakfast together and you ask me if I can reach the salt, and I can, I will probably grab it and pass it to you. If I can't I may in turn ask someone sitting closer to it to do so. If we have been talking about the effects of my tennis elbow on my ability to extend my arm, however, I may simply try to touch the salt and let you observe whether I can or can't, and how much exertion and suffering it requires. If you are closer to the salt, I might think you are assuming I can't reach the salt, and probably want some salt, and so are offering to pass it to me. I infer from your asking to your mental state; I try to figure out what your reason for asking was, and how I might fit into your plans. My inference will not be based solely on what you say, but also on what larger activity it is a part of, what I know about you, what I think you know about me, and so on. I am using context not to disambiguate your words or syntax, or to determine what pronouns or other indexicals stand for, but to determine what you are doing with words. You reasoning, in choosing what to say, is a species of practical reasoning. We say things for reasons, and choose what we say in order to advance our plans. My reasoning, in figuring out what you are trying to do, is a species of inference to the best explanation. Context in pragmatics is simply circumstances that are relevant to planning the effects of an utterance, and inferring from an utterance to the plan that led to it.

The co-reference and no-reference problems can be seen as an apparent failure on the part of referentialism to provide us with what we need to understanding the planning that leads to the production of utterances and the inferences that result from understanding utterances. If 'I am John Perry' and 'John Perry is John Perry' express the same proposition, why do I use the first to tell you my name and not the second? If you ask no question when you say, "Who is Santa Claus" and I say nothing when I respond, "He brings presents on Christmas eve," then why is this a satisfactory exchange rather than nonsense?

The reflexive-referential theory holds that the failure is merely apparent. A semantics that is directed towards providing the referential truth-conditions will in fact provide a broad, useful, and straightforward interface to pragmatics, conceived as the study of practical reasoning and inference to the best explanation applied to language. The issues covered in the book hardly constitute an impressive case for this conception of pragmatics, for the focus is rather narrow, on a set of problem cases and a certain approach to semantics. My hope is that if a certain prejudice is removed, which I call 'the subject matter fallacy', this conception will become quite attractive. The subject matter fallacy is supposing that the content of a statement or a belief is wholly constituted by the conditions its truth puts on the subject matter of the statement or belief; that is, the conditions it puts on the objects the words designate or the ideas are of.

One final word about these different kinds of or concepts of context. The application is not linear. Usually if you and I are having breakfast with an old sea-captain and you ask, "Can you pass the salt," I will take you to be using 'salt' with the meaning of table salt, not with the meaning veteran seafarer. If I'm just arriving for breakfast, and the old captain's wheelchair is positioned so that I have to squeeze between it and the wall to get to my seat, I may take you to mean veteran seafarer by 'salt', and to be offering to move the chair if necessary. (I would probably also take you to be making a pun.) One of the factors that helps us disambiguate words, and resolve the reference of pronouns, and supplement content, is the overall purpose we attribute to the speaker.

4

Context and cognitive paths

4.1 Introduction

A central function of cognition is helping us to handle information. We use our senses to pick up information about the world we live in with through our senses, and use the information to guide our action. Communication allows us to share information, so we can guide our actions by information that others have acquired, and others can make use of information we have acquired. Language provides us with tools for such information exchanges.

These tools have to allow us to identify the objects and facts in the world that we have knowledge about. This aspect of language accords with referentialism. But communication requires more than this. We have to identify objects in ways that permit our listeners to identify them, and to recognize them as objects they have encountered in other circumstances, so they can pool old and new information. There may seem to be a tension between these two aspects of language, but there is not. The very meanings that allow us to identify external objects and state external facts provide us with rich resources for planning our utterances so as to achieve communication.

In this chapter, I show how the meanings of indexicals allow speakers to plan cognitive paths suitable to different contexts. These paths enable us to get information we want to share to those with whom we want to share it a useful way.

4.2 Information games

I think many parents and grandparents have had this experience. You are driving on a trip and it is time for lunch. You are happy enough to leave the choice to the kids sitting in the back seat; they want you to turn into the first McDonald's that comes along. You'll keep your mind on the traffic while they look for one. As you maneuver through a complex intersection you hear a shout, "That's a McDonald's." One of the children has said something, probably perfectly unambiguous and clear. She has expressed a singular proposition,

A is a McDonald's

where **A** is the building at which she points. You have the power to turn into the McDonald's and make the children happy. But it does no good. You can't see where she is pointing; you don't know what she is telling you to do; you go through the intersection, the McDonald's slips away; tears ensue.

This example illustrates a couple of concepts that are central to this chapter. The first is that of an *information game*. An information game is defined by two episodes: (i) someone picks up some information at a given time about a particular person, thing or place; (ii) someone uses that information to guide action at some time. In the simplest information game, what I call the 'straight through' game, steps (i) and (ii) involve the same person and the same time. I'm thirsty; I see a glass of water, I pick it up and drink it. In more complex games, the times and the people differ. In the episode with the children, things didn't go right. A child in the back seat picked up some information, that a certain building, visible from there, was occupied by a McDonald's restaurant. The idea was that that information would be transmitted to you, and would guide your behavior—you would turn down the street where the McDonald's was to be found.

The fact that things did not work illustrates a second point. Indexicals give us ways of referring to things. The way they refer to things, makes them tools suited for some purposes and not others. 'That' is a word we can use to refer to something that is *salient*. It can be a thing or a place that has just been spoken of:

> 'I'm going to City Hall';

> 'That's a place I've never been'.

It can also be a thing that the speaker is attending to or pointing to, as it was in the case with the children. There is no doubt that the child referred to just the place he intended to, the place he was looking at. The problem was that you were not in a position to see where he was looking, or to follow any demonstration he might provide. The word 'that' isn't a good tool for conveying information about a place to someone for whom the place is not salient from previous conversation, and who cannot easily find out which place the speaker is attending to or demonstrating. So in this case you didn't get the information; the information game didn't work.

The child managed to express the relevant proposition, that a certain building was occupied by a suitable eatery. There is no reason to deny that she said that. If it had been a Burger King or a Wendy's rather than a McDonald's, her siblings would have chided her for saying something false. You understood her words. You may even have had a clear understanding of what was happening: that the child was looking out one or the other of the rear windows, was focussing on a building, was referring to it with 'that' and was saying of it that it was occupied by a McDonald's. The problem is that you did not grasp what she said in the right way to influence your action.

To drive towards the McDonald's in the way that the child wanted you to, you needed to locate the building in your visual field, so that you know which way to turn the wheel, and how far, and when to stop turning once you were going in the right direction. Knowing where the place is relative to the child — that is in her line of vision — won't enable you to steer to the place, although it might have helped you find the place in your own field of vision if you had more time and the freedom to turn and see where her gaze led. Had the child been a better communicator, she would have realized this; she would have seen that her plan, for getting the information she wanted you to act on to you, had a gap in it.

4.3 Cognitive paths

A skilled communicator will have some conception of a *cognitive path* that can lead from the way he thinks of the object about which he has information, to the way in which the listener must think about it, to act in the way that the speaker wants to bring about.[17] Had the child been such a skilled communicator, she might have said, "Mom, when you have a moment, look off to your right, out the passenger side window, and you'll see a street. Down that street is a building; it is occupied a McDonald's." But kids seldom plan that way or talk that way. In an act of communication, the cognitive path the speaker has in mind for the listener to follow (however implicitly), leads from the utterance to some notion that the listener has of the object that is relevant to the change in the belief the speaker wants to bring about. *Notion* is my term for the ideas we have of people, things and places. Notions are concrete particulars, though not necessarily simple ones. The philosopher David Lewis carries three by five inch note cards in his shirt pocket; he pulls them out to jot down information, ideas, and the like. My image of a notion is just a ghostly internal version of David Lewis's cards; little cards in the mind on which we jot down information about people, things and places. My picture is a card for each person, place, or thing. (I don't claim that's exactly the way Lewis uses his cards, however.) Perhaps little mental file folders is a better metaphor. Perhaps some picture associated with a fancier way of keeping track of information, a spread-sheet, say, or some other sort of relational data-base would be even better (See Crimmins, 1992).

These notions can be *attached* to perceptions, or be *detached*. My notion of David Lewis, for example, was formed when I met him at UCLA in 1967; it was attached to my perceptions then,

---

[17]See Taylor, 1993 on 'Ancillary Anchoring Routes'.

as I shook his hand and studied his looks; it has been attached at various times since then when I have met him, but most of the time it has been detached. Detached notions are useful to us, if they are associated with enough information to allow us to recognize the person or thing or place they are of, so we can apply the information on a subsequent encounter. The *detach-and-recognize* information game, in fact, is the basis of much of our cognitive architecture, and of much of the way we talk about cognition (Perry, 1997a).

Suppose now that a Stanford student is off to Princeton for a job interview. The student has a notion of David Lewis, acquired through reading and absorbing the lore of philosophy, but has never seen him. She has a David Lewis file, associated with such ideas as having written a number of important books, inventing counterpart theory, and so forth. She flies to Newark, takes the train to Princeton, and David meets her at the train station. He says,

(20)   I am David Lewis.

The proposition he expresses is of course quite trivial, on the referentialist scheme of things; it is a necessary proposition:

(P^{r}20)   That **David Lewis** is **David Lewis**.

Nevertheless, the utterance is an effective way of getting a bit of contingent information to the student: who it is that has come to meet her.

Let us suppose that Lewis assumes that the student has a notion of him; that is, that she has a notion that is associated with such ideas as being named 'David Lewis', teaching at Princeton, being interested in possible worlds, and the like. He knows that she will be comfortable knowing to whom she is talking, and the conversation will be more interesting and productive if it can be guided by her knowledge about him, as well as his knowledge about her. The word 'I' refers to David Lewis, as do the words 'David Lewis'. But the word 'I' refers to Lewis in virtue of the fact that he says it. As a result the student knows, when Lewis says 'I', that the person to whom he refers is the person speaking to her, and so the person in front of her, the person she will be speaking to when she speaks. The name 'David Lewis', on the other hand, refers to David Lewis in virtue of his having been given that name. She knows, then, that for the utterance to be true, the person in front of her must be named 'David Lewis'. Given her circumstances, she can infer that he is in fact the David Lewis she knows about; although 'David Lewis' is probably a pretty common name, there is likely to be only one in the Princeton Philosophy Department. If there were another person with this name who had been sent to meet the student, he would no doubt say something like, 'not *that* David Lewis'. Thus her actions towards the person in front of her can be guided by the information she has associated with her David Lewis notion. So she will smile, say something like, 'I've wanted to meet you for a long time', and shake hands.

On referentialist principles, Lewis could have said the same thing, expressed the same proposition, by saying 'I am I' or 'David Lewis is David Lewis'. But neither of these would have done the trick of getting the student to realize that the person in front of her was the well-known philosopher. Lewis's choice of words, then, shows a good plan for his listener's cognitive path.

The listener's or reader's cognitive path starts with the perception of a token. Sometimes the perception of a token is accompanied by the perception of the utterance which produces it, as when David extends his hand and says, 'I am David Lewis'. At other times, the utterance must be inferred, as when I receive a postcard, or a note, or email. A phone call might be thought of either way. If we think of 'hearing-on-the-phone' as a form of perception, then we might say that I am perceiving, hearing the utterance, as well as the token produced. But if we think of a phone call as a complex process, in which what is delivered to the ear of the listener is a copy of the original token, we might think of the utterance as inferred. By 'inference' here I do not mean a slow and deliberate process of ratiocination, but refer to the grounds of the belief that the token is the product of an utterance.

While my explanations of notions and ideas use metaphors like file cards, file-folders, and the like, underlying the metaphors are two facts that I think justify us in postulating notions and reasoning with them and about them. First is that every system we know about that is capable of picking up information about an individual, and manipulating, combining, and storing it so that it is available for later use in dealing with that individual, involves some such (relatively) concrete particulars to unify the representations of the various bits of information about the object. Second, it is clear that belief in such ideas is a part of folk psychology that we all use in dealing with one another. We would talk freely about the idea the graduate student formed of David Lewis when she read works by and about him, how she used this idea to recognize the man who met her as the philosopher David Lewis; how her idea developed as time went by. We could readily recognize the possibility that she had two unconnected ideas of the same person—if say David Lewis happened to be a friend's uncle whom she met years ago and remembered, but never realized was the famous philosopher. My talk of notions and ideas is simply an attempt to regiment our thinking and talking about the ideas we all recognize people to have, in a way that will keep any theoretical commitments modest and explicit.

It has become common in our century to think of any structure or system of representations, or content bearing states of any kind, as a 'language'. Rather than talking with Locke and Hume about ideas and notions, the thoroughly modern philosopher tends to talk of the language of thought. I avoid this. I don't know very much about the mental structures, and what I think I know comes from having a view about how they are used to store and process information. Better to call them by names they have had for centuries, like 'ideas', 'notions', and 'thoughts', than to borrow terms for linguistic structures and events. Languages, in the literal sense, are systems humans use for communicating with one another. We produce tokens of various types, counting on humans to recognize these and learn thereby what we are thinking, or at least what we want them to think. This is not true of ideas and notions. They may turn out to be publically observable perturbations of the brain, but if so this fact about them is not the key to their utility. Finally, we do often use language in talking to ourselves. It is useful to do this in a variety of situations: in deliberating about problems where the resources of a natural language are helpful in clarifying things; in urging, encouraging, scolding, and admiring ourselves; in rehearsing what we are going to say; in going over what we should have said. For most of us our first language is our language of thought in this sense, even when we are in situation in which we must converse in some other language. It seems to me that using language in this way requires other, prior representational system for keeping track of facts, imagining possibilities, deliberating among options and planning actions. It seems unwise to think of this prior structure as a language without some clear reason for supposing it is similar to what we ordinarily call languages. So I prefer the old-fashioned terminology of ideas, notions, concepts, and the like, until something clearly better comes along.

4.4   Indexicals and contexts

Various indexicals and demonstratives fit well into common conversational situations. They are multi-purpose tools, but they are not all-purpose tools. In classifying indexicals and their contexts I'll emphasize two distinctions, which together create the four categories exhibited in Table 1:

Does designation depend on narrow or wide context?

Is designation 'automatic' given meaning and public contextual facts, or does it depend in part on the intentions of the speaker?

I'll show which expressions seem to fit into these categories, and then explain them:

TABLE 1: TYPES OF INDEXICALS

	Narrow	**Wide**
Automatic	I, now*, here*, tomorrow	yea, dthat(α),
Discretionary	now, here	that, this man, there, he, she, it (used demonstratively or for anaphoric co-designation)

Narrow and wide context. Any indexical will identify an object by a role that it plays in the lives of the speaker and his listeners. And all of these roles will in some way connect with the utterance the speaker makes, for this is the starting point of the cognitive paths on which the speaker relies. But given that, the roles vary tremendously in how intimately they are related to the utterance. They vary, that is, in the extent to which their designation depends not simply on the essential facts about the utterance, but on various other things somehow related to the speaker and listeners at the time of utterance.

What I call the *narrow context* consists of facts about which things occupy the essential roles involved in the utterance, which I will take to be the agent, time and position. These roles are filled with every utterance. The clearest case of an indexical that relies only on the narrow context is 'I', whose designation depends on the agent and nothing else. The *wide context* consists of those facts, plus anything else that might be relevant, according to the workings of a particular indexical.

The sorts of factors on which an indexical can be made to depend seem, in principle, limitless. For example,

It is yea big.

means that it is as big as the space between the outstretched hands of the speaker, so this space is a contextual factor in the required sense for the indexical 'yea'.[18]

---

[18]This word is a familiar part of what I think of as standard American English, i.e., that dialect of English spoken in Nebraska. I have been informed it is not very common in certain more obscure dialects of English, spoken in the United Kingdom and on the eastern coast of America.

Automatic versus discretionary indexicals. When Rip Van Winkle says, "I fell asleep yesterday," he intended to designate (let us suppose), July 3, 1766. He in fact designated July 2, 1786, for he awoke twenty years to the day after he fell asleep. An utterance of 'yesterday' designates the day before the utterance occurs, no matter what the speaker intends. Given the meaning and context, the designation is automatic. No further intention, than that of using the words with their ordinary meaning, is relevant.

The designation of an utterance of 'that man', however, is not automatic. The speaker's intention is relevant. There may be several men standing across the street when I say, 'That man stole my wallet'. Which of them I refer to depends on my intention. I have some choice or discretion in the matter.

However, we need to be careful here. Suppose there are two men across the street, Harold dressed in brown and Fred in blue. I think that Harold stole my wallet and I also think wrongly that the man dressed in blue is Harold. I intend to designate Harold *by* designating the man in blue. So I point towards the man in blue as I say 'that man'. In this case I designate the man in blue—even if my pointing is a bit off target. My intention to point to the man in blue is relevant to the issue of whom I designate, and what I say, but my intention to refer to Harold is not. In this case, I say something I don't intend to say, that Fred, the man in blue, stole my wallet, and fail say what I intended to, that Harold did. So it is not just any referential intention that is relevant to demonstratives, but only the more basic ones, which I will call *directing intentions*, following Kaplan (1989b).

I take a directing intention to be the intention to refer to an object X simply in virtue of the meanings of one's words and the context, both pre-existing and supplied by the speaker. This sense of directing intentions applies to all indexicals, even 'I'. If I say "I" I intend to refer to myself simply in virtue of the meaning of 'I' in English and the fact that I am speaking. Assuming I have my wits about me I also intend to refer to John Perry. If I lose my wits I may intend to refer to Napoleon. Elsewhere I have labelled 'intentional' the category here labelled 'discretionary'. The word 'intentional' now seems misleading. The real point isn't whether or not there is an intention; even with 'I' one must have the intention, however implicit, to be using the word with the meaning it has in English. The issue is whether one's lowest level intention can have an effect on what one designates.

The indexicals 'I', 'now', and 'here' are often given an honored place as 'pure' or 'essential' indexicals. Some writers emphasize the possibility of translating away other indexicals in favor of them[19] In Table 1, this honored place is represented by the cell labelled 'narrow' and 'automatic'. However, it is doubtful that 'now' and 'here' deserve this status, hence the asterisks. With 'here' there is the question of how large an area is to count, and with 'now' the question of how large a stretch of time. If I say, "I left my pen here," I would be taken to designate a relatively small area, say the office in which I was looking. If I say, "The evenings are cooler than you expect here" I might mean to include the whole San Francisco Bay area. In 'Now that we walk upright, we have lots of back problems,' 'now' would seem to designate a large if indefinite period of time that includes the very instant of utterance, while in 'Why did you wait until now to tell me?' it seems to designate a considerably smaller stretch. It seems then that these indexicals really have an discretionary element.

'Today,' 'yesterday' and 'tomorrow', however, seem automatic. 'Today' designates a twenty-four hour stretch of time, midnight to midnight, that includes the time of the utterance. Which twenty-four hour stretch of time depends on the place of the utterance as well as the time. It also depends on the time-zone, whether daylight-savings time is in effect, and so forth. If one thinks of those facts as fixed by the time and place, these terms belong in the narrow cell; if one thinks of them as much a matter of politics as geography, one might move these terms over the the 'wide' cell.

'Here' can be used as a demonstrative, when used to contrast

---

[19]See Castañeda, 1967, Corazza, 1995.

with 'there'. You are trying to point out a bird on a distant tree to a companion standing on your right. They are looking too far to the right, and you say, "No not there, over here," pointing to a distant tree. One can also point to a place on a map and refer to it as 'here', as in, 'Let's go here next summer' (Kaplan, 1989a).

To have an intention to do something is often thought to require that one can do that thing, or at least thinks that one can do it, or at least thinks that one has a chance of doing it. If there is an man across the street that I see, but no one else does, can I refer to it with 'he' or 'that man'? Perhaps it is not so clear. I can certainly use this phrase in thinking or talking to myself. But if I intend to secure uptake on the part of my listeners, and them to think of the person to whom I am at least trying to refer, I must do something to make the man *salient*. So I may point or otherwise demonstrate the person. But if the man is already salient, this won't be necessary.

There are a variety of familiar ways that objects can be salient, so that a speaker can hope to draw attention of his listeners to them in order to convey information about them. That is, there are a number of familiar ways of constructing cognitive paths so that there is some obvious step to take after perceiving the utterance. Each path starts with a role that the object in question is playing (or the speaker thinks it is playing) relative to the utterance.

> In anaphoric co-designation, an object can be salient as the designation of a thread in the conversation of which the utterance is a part; I can refer to the object by using a pronoun with an earlier noun-phrase in the thread as its antecedent; I need to be able to employ, and my listeners need to be able to detect, the various ways in which antecedency is conveyed.

> An object can be salient as the object that some or most of the audience of the utterance is perceiving or can be encouraged to perceive.

> An object can be salient as the object associated by some

relation with some object that is already salient to the audience of the utterance. There is an large noise and I say "That firecracker was a big one." I ask you for dinner on a certain day and you say "That week is impossible for me." The speaker needs to get his audience to grasp which salient object and which relation are in question.

An object can be salient as the object that the speaker is perceiving or otherwise interacting with. I am talking to you on the phone, and I say "this pencil is broken. Hold the line."

4.5 Stretch the dog

The role of directing intentions in the use of demonstratives can be understood in terms of the concept of a cognitive path. Let's consider the picture on the front cover of this book.[20] (Readers of the cloth edition please refer to the last page in the book.) This is a picture of the veranda of the Stanford Bookstore, with a dog's head emerging from one side of a pillar, and a dog's behind and tail emerging from the other side. It looks like it could be one very long dog, partly obscured by the pillar. (At times—including this one— we'll imagine that there is only one long dog there, and I'll use the name 'Stretch' for it.) Suppose I point first at the head of the dog in front, and then at the tail of the dog in the rear, using the same phrase, 'that dog' with each demonstration: I ask, "Do you think that dog is that dog?" Even though I refer to Stretch twice, and use the same phrase twice with the same meaning, I can clearly reasonably expect these two acts of reference to have different cognitive effects on the listener in a position to see my utterance. That is, I plan on him hearing two tokens of 'that dog', seeing two different utterances, having his attention directed towards two different parts of the scene or picture, having two different perceptions, and establishing two different buffers, at

[20]I've moved from the battleships (Perry, 1970, Perry, 1977) to dogs partly to give the book a less militaristic air but mainly because I like this picture by Linda Cicero.

least temporarily, to keep track of what I am going to tell him and what he is going to observe about however many dogs there turn out to be. By having two notions my listener will not be judging that there are two dogs; he will merely be failing to judge that there is but one, the reasonable thing to do, given this scene.

This is quite a different effect than saying something like "Do you think that dog is not self-identical," with only one demonstration, or "Do you think that dog is not the same as that one" with two exactly similar demonstrations to the head.

Assume that there is but one dog in the picture, Stretch. Then both utterances of 'that dog' designate Stretch, even though one is accompanied by a point to his head, the other to his tail. If we suppose that the 'semantic value' of a demonstrative is the object it designates, then we seem to have a problem. If both utterances have the words with the same meaning and the same designation, how can they, in virtue of their semantics, have different cognitive effects? Because the cognitive path doesn't begin with the common meaning or common designation, but with different tokens used by different utterances. These utterances are similar, but not indiscernible, and the condition a dog has to satisfy to be the referent of the first is not the same as it has to satisfy to be the referent of the second.

You hear me say, "that dog." You know that I produced the token you hear, and know that that the referent will be a dog that I am attending to and seeking to direct the attention of my chosen listeners to.

If you are among the people that I intend to be imparting information to, and I am a reasonably adroit speaker, you will expect me to give you some directions to pick out the dog I have in mind. You will expect me to point, with my hands or perhaps merely by directing my gaze, in a way that invites to do the same. You will expect to have a perception to attach to the buffer you set up for the dog to whom I refer, with which you can associate the various dog attributes you pick up from the perception. The dog or dog part I want you to attend to must be perceptually or in some other way sufficiently *salient* for you to start down the cognitive path I plan for you. We'll return to Stretch in the next chapter.

4.6 Dthat

In 'Dthat', David Kaplan introduces a new demonstrative, 'that'. I'll explain how this new demonstrative works in my terminology. Suppose 'α' is a definite description, that designates x. Then 'that(α)' also designates x. But whereas 'α' *describes*, 'that(α)' *refers*. That is, 'that(α)' contributes x itself, rather than the identifying condition, being α, to the propositions expressed by statements of which it is a part.[21]

I have included 'that' in the cell for indexicals that are automatic and wide. 'Dthat' is automatic, because it refers to the object designated by 'α,' with no discretionary role for the speaker's directing intentions. It is wide because it can incorporate any fact whatsoever into context. Pick any fact, a definite description can be framed the denotation of which turns on the fact. Then Kaplan's new demonstrative converts that fact to a part of the context.

'Dthat' is a perfectly coherent demonstrative, for Kaplan's rules are clear and consistent. Still, there is something out of the spirit of indexicality about it. Familiar indexicals and demonstratives are tools for constructing cognitive paths from objects that play, or can be easily made to play, certain roles in the conversational situation to notions of them in the minds of the listeners or readers. There is typically some sort of relative limited accessibility. Only one person can refer to David Kaplan as 'I'; we can refer to noon, April 15, 2000 as 'now' only at that time; we can refer to an object demonstratively only if we can perceive it, or remember it, or it has already been made salient in the conversation.

In contrast, names and descriptions allow us to designate objects that play no immediate role in our conversation, are not

---

[21]Note that in the language of this book, putting a description into boldface but not into italics functions like 'dthat'.

perceivable by the participants, and have not been made salient by previous conversation. 'Dthat' seems more like names and descriptions than like other indexicals and demonstratives in this regard. The 'cognitive load' that names, descriptions, indexicals and demonstratives put on the listener and user are typically rather different. As we shall see in more gruesome detail later, this is the reason Israel chooses to use his own name, and not the first person pronoun 'I', when talking to the government bureaucrat.

4.7 Real, doxastic and fictional contexts

The main campus of Stanford University and the adjacent lands that Stanford owns are almost all in Santa Clara County, California. But a little part of Stanford's golf course is on the north side of San Francisquito Creek, and thus a part of San Mateo County.

Many golfers don't know this. Consider this conversation between two such ignorant duffers:

> I received a jury notice from the county court. Where do I have to go?
> San Jose is the county seat of this county.

The second golfer refers to San Mateo County, and says something false. By doing so, he managed to convey something true to the first golfer, however. The second golfer intended to say, and convey, the proposition that San Jose was the county seat of Santa Clara County; the first golfer came to believe this true proposition, and presumably made it to his jury assignment.

This sort of case may tempt us to suppose that the contexts that are relevant to communication, semantics, pragmatics and the study of language are not facts about the real world, but facts about the beliefs of those who are using the language. On this view, we should think of contexts as mental representations of the environment of the utterance. Both golfers believed that that their conversation was taking place in Santa Clara County. If we use such a doxastic context instead of the real context to determine what they said, we would get the seemingly welcome result that the golfer said what he meant to say, and was properly understood.

I don't think this is the right way to look at things. But surely it has an important point. It is what a person believes the context of an utterance to be that effects his interpretation of the utterance, and it would be foolish to suppose otherwise. Moreover, we often use language to change a person's beliefs about the context, or to suppose or imagine something about the context, rather than about the subject matter.

Still, there are many cases where mistakes about context don't cancel themselves out in the way they do in this one, and in such cases the temptation to consider only 'doxastic context' vanishes. To take an extreme case, suppose that someone today believes himself to be Napoleon. When this person says, "I won a very big battle at Austerlitz," he intends to be expressing a true proposition, that Napoleon won a very big battle at Austerlitz, by expressing a true proposition about himself. He thinks he can do this, because he thinks he is Napoleon, the place Waterloo and the time 1815. But the fact that he intends to be expressing a true proposition about Napoleon should not lead us to say that he does so. Given that Napoleon is long dead, we can be quite sure that the speaker is not Napoleon. If the speaker is not Napoleon, he did not succeed in referring to Napoleon by referring to himself. And he certainly did not win the battle of Austerlitz. Therefore, when he says that he did, he is wrong. We need his incorrect representation of the context to explain *why* he says something false, but we need the real context in which he speaks to explain *that* he said something false.

Although it is the real context that is relevant to what speakers say, surely it is the doxastic context that is relevant to understanding why they say it, and predicting what they will say next. And we can learn about a person's beliefs about the doxastic context, about the situation they take themselves to be in, by seeing how they use context-dependent terms. The golfer above either had false beliefs about which county he was in, or about what the county seat of San Mateo County. If we are confident that he wouldn't have been so ignorant as to think that San Jose was the county seat of San Mateo County, we can be sure he was mistaken about in which county the bit of land on which he stands lies.

Suppose now that the first golfer is actually aware that they are in San Mateo County. He is quite sure, however, that his partner knows which counties have which county seats. He would ignore what his partner actually said, and focus on the true belief that partly motivated it. That is, he would suppose that his partner said "San Jose is the county seat of this county" because he believed that San Jose was the county seat of Santa Clara County and wrongly thought he was in Santa Clara County. The first golfer can thus learn what he wants to know from the second golfer's remark, even if the second golfer's remark was false.

Perhaps the first golfer feels obliged to correct his partner's geographical mistake. One way to do that would be to say "The county seat of this county is Redwood City." The statement does not mention the golfers, but it will convey to the second golfer that the golfers are not in Santa Clara County but in San Mateo County. Here the first golfer assumes that the second golfer is confused about which county they are in, but has his facts about county seats straight. The second golfer can figure out that for what the first golfer says to be true, they must be standing in San Mateo County and not in Santa Clara County.

Suppose now I am an energetic history teacher. The class has been covering the Napoleonic Wars. I want to make sure they are reading their assignments. I say,

> OK, who am I? It's now 1815; I'm short, I'm looking at my horse that has just been shot, I'm looking at the Prussians arriving on my flank, and I'm watching the English beat my army in the valley below. Who am I?

The students, of course, are supposed to say, "You are Napoleon." In this case I didn't really think that I was Napoleon or that it was 1815; I was testing them on their homework by seeing if they knew who would have to be talking to them, if the statement they heard was true—who I was pretending to be.

The example comes from Quentin Smith (1989) who thinks we need to postulate new special meanings for 'I' or 'now' in this case. But if we do, we might not be able to explain the way the test works. The students are challenged, so to speak, to solve for context, given facts and the ordinary meanings of 'I' and 'now'.

Had he been in an impish mood, David Lewis might have done something similar with our student. Instead of saying "I am David Lewis" he might have said: "I am the only member of the Princeton Department with a B.A. from Oberlin. Who am I?" The student would have to solve for context. The difference is that the teaching method in the history class involved pretending. Note that even with David's original utterance, 'I am David Lewis', the fundamental mechanism of figuring out context from content is working. The difference is simply that figuring out who the person you are talking to has to be, to truthfully and appropriately say 'I am David Lewis' isn't too tricky.

5

Meanings and Contents

5.1 Introduction

As I use the term, *meanings* are the rules language associates with simple and complex expressions-types. These rules may be equisignificant, and assign the same content to each utterance of a given expression. Or they may exploit contextual factors, and assign different contents to different utterances of the same expression. So *content* is an attribute of individual utterances, as determined by those rules, which may or may not exploit contextual factors.

Even with equisignificant languages, the meaning-content distinction is worth making. The meaning is the rule language associates with an expression, the content what we get when we follow the rule.

If we construct a sort of 'vanilla' semantics for simple atomic sentences of equisignificant languages, it will help us to see the changes that will be required when we add indexicals. Our vanilla semantics will have three levels, meaning, content and designation.

The atomic sentences of our language will be in the style of the predicate calculus:

(21) $\phi(\tau_1, \ldots, \tau_n)$

where ϕ is a relation symbol and each τ_i is a name, indexical or definite description.

The content (Con) of an utterance of an atomic sentence is a structured proposition. The content of (21) is the proposition:

(P21) $\langle Con(u_\phi), \langle Con(u_{\tau_1}), \dots, Con(u_{\tau_n}) \rangle \rangle$

The contents of the utterances of terms will be either individuals, if the terms are names, or identifying conditions, if they are descriptions.

The content of a statement is a proposition, incorporating the conditions of truth of the statement. The designation of a statement is its truth-value. The content of a predicate (for our purposes, a declarative sentence with some of its terms replaced by variables) is a condition on objects. The designation of a predicate is the set of n-tuples of objects that meet the condition. The content of a definite description is a identifying condition; its designation the individual that fits that condition. The content of a name is an individual, and so is the designation; for names content and designation coincide. The contents of terms combine with the contents of utterances of predicates to yield propositions.

This vanilla semantics captures what is common to various important schemes. In Frege's system, sinn corresponds to content, and bedeutung to designation.[22] Although Frege called many expressions proper names, he didn't give any of them a treatment corresponding to the Table 2 account of proper names. Proper names in his languages are assigned identifying conditions. In possible worlds semantics, intension corresponds to content and extension to designation. Russell's meaning corresponds to Table 2's content, (if we set aside his view that descriptions really are not meaningful units).

Indexicals can be fit directly into this picture, by allowing the meanings associated with types to be rules that assign content relative to context. This is more or less that path followed by David Kaplan in 'Demonstratives'. His concept of *character* is close to that of meaning in my sense; characters are functions or rules associated by language with *types*.

Burks, however, introduces an additional level to deal with

---

[22]To avoid problems of translation, I use 'sinn' and 'bedeutung' as English words, with the plurals 'sinne' and 'bedeutungen'.

TABLE 2: Vanilla Semantics for an Equisignificant Language

	If α is a name	If α is a description	If α is an n-place predicate	If α is a sentence
the Meaning of α is	a rule associating α with an individual	a rule associating α with an identifying condition	a rule associating α with an n-ary condition on individuals	a rule associating α with a proposition
the Content of utterance of α	an individual	an identifying condition	an n-ary condition on individuals	a proposition
the Designation of utterance of α is	an individual	an individual	a set of n-tuples	a truth-value

indexicals, aspect (iv) of section 3.2 above, which he calls the 'indexical meaning' of the token. This is the result of combining the meaning of the type with the specific token. At this level it is the token itself, not the existential facts about it, that come into play. Perhaps the simplest way to grasp this idea and its potential importance is to imagine seeing a token or hearing a token without being in a position to perceive the existential facts or context. For example, you find a note that says, "I plan to kill him tomorrow." You don't know who wrote it, in reference to whom, and when. You have the token, but not the context. So you grasp what Burks calls the indexical meaning. Because you grasp that, you may be highly motivated to find out the existential facts—it may be relevant to saving someone's life. The proposition you have grasped in something like,

> That the author of **this note** did kill or will kill the person to whom the token of 'he' refers on the day following the day when it was written.

This is not the proposition expressed by the note, but it is an important proposition. It is reflexive, in that it is a proposition *about* the note *itself*.

This level does not appear in Table 2. In Kaplan's approach to indexicals, the level of analysis represented by Burks's aspect (iv) is bypassed. The meaning, or *character*, of an indexical is, on Kaplan's theory, a function from context to content, to what is said. No intervening level of content is recognized. The approach Jon Barwise and I took in *Situations and Attitudes* (1983) was similar to Kaplan's, although we did compensate somewhat with what we called 'inverse interpretation'. Stalnaker (1981) complained that something was missing from such approaches, and I have come to think that he and Burks were correct. In fact, we need an intermediate level of content.

Although I follow Burks in recognizing the need for this intermediate level, I don't quite adopt his terminology. I will henceforth call the content of Table 2 *referential* content. In addition to meaning, referential content and designation, I recognize *indexical content.* Since it is a property of utterances rather than types, it is in line with my terminology to call this level 'content', although it corresponds to Burks's 'indexical meaning'. Indexical content is *reflexive* content, in that reflexive identifying conditions are incorporated into content. The indexical content incorporates the objects associated by the rules of language with an expression. The meanings are fixed. If we assume that names *name*, then fixing the meaning fixes the referent in the case of names. But fixing the meaning only fixes the identifying condition in the case of denoting expressions, such as indexicals and descriptions.

At the level of referential content the semantic contextual facts, those relevant to the references of indexicals, are also fixed. So the referential content of an expression incorporates the objects *referred to* by referring expressions—names and indexicals. Using the terminology of chapter 2, we can say that for indexicals, the referential content is the indexical content *loaded* by the contextual facts.

I call my account of indexicals the reflexive-*referential* account, because it recognizes levels of content of both sort. Indexical content is reflexive, and reflexive contents of various sorts are my candidates for the *cognitive significance* of expressions. Referential content is my candidate for 'what is said' or *official content*.

Referential content does not quite correspond to Burks's concept of 'the information conveyed by a sign'. I recognize a level that does correspond to Burks's concept, which I call *designational content*. To get from referential content to designational content we load the identifying conditions that are the contents of descriptions by the facts about the designata of those descriptions. Designational content provides one way of interpreting Donnellan's 'referential' uses of definite descriptions (setting aside the issue of 'near misses'). If I say "Jones' murderer is insane" the referential content (using my terminology) is that **Jones'** *murderer* is insane; the designational content is **Jones' murderer** is insane–that is, if Smith murdered Jones, that **Smith** is insane. My designational content lines up with Donnellan's referential use of the phrase 'Jones' murderer'; referential content lines up with the attributive use of the descriptions. The mismatch in terminology is due to the fact that I am using 'reference' only for the type of designation that names and indexicals have.

Now I will try to quickly give a sense of picture that motivates this framework, explain the some details, and provide some arguments for looking at things this way.

5.2 Reichenbach, reflexivity and indexical content

To explain the reflexive-referential account, I need to explain the reflexive part and the referential part. In the rest of this chapter I explain the difference between the two kinds of content, and explain the importance of indexical content.

Reflexivity was once a major theme in the study of indexicals. Reichenbach put forward a *token-reflexive* theory in his *Elements of Symbolic Logic* (1947). He thought that the meanings of tokens of indexicals and demonstratives involved the tokens themselves, which explained how different tokens of the same type could stand for different things.[23]

Reichenbach claimed that token-reflexive words could be defined in terms of the token-reflexive phrase 'this token', and in particular, as he put it, "The word 'I' ... means the same as 'the person who utters this token' ..."(284). He used this idea to provide an account of a famous utterance:

> ... let us symbolize the sentence 'here I stand', uttered by Luther on the Reichstag at Worms in 1521. The utterance by Luther we denote by 'θ'. The word 'I' then can be given in the form 'the x that spoke θ'; the word 'here'will be expressed by the phrase 'the place z where θ was spoken'. We thus have, using the function 'x speaks y at z', with 'sp'for 'speak'and 'st' for 'stand'...
> $$st[(\iota x)(Ez)sp(x,\theta,z),(\iota z)(Ex)sp(x,\theta,z)]$$

---

[23]I do not attempt to explain everything Reichenbach had in mind. He called token-reflexive words 'pseudo-phrases', since different tokens of the same symbol (type) are not equisignificant. He desired to symbolize the meanings of sentences in which they occur in a properly-behaved metalanguage, which he thought would not contain token-reflexives.

If we take Reichenbach's claim as a literal claim of synonymy between 'I' and 'the person who utters this token', it is wrong. The two terms may be assigned the same condition, but 'I' refers whereas 'the person who utters this token' describes. But Reichenbach was clearly on to something. There is an intimate connection between the meanings of 'I' and 'the person who utters this token', even if it falls short of synonymy. The second phrase does not *have* the meaning of 'I', but it *gives* part of the meaning of 'I'. It supplies the condition of designation that English associates with 'I'. We can put this in a way that brings out the reflexivity:

> If u is an utterance of 'I', the condition of designation for u is *being the speaker of* **u**.

Here we see that the condition of designation assigned to an utterance u has that very utterance as a constituent, hence it is reflexive. (I discussed the reasons for using 'utterance' rather than 'token' above in the last chapter.)

As I said, meaning belongs to types, content to specific utterances. Let u be a specific utterance of 'I'. When we take u together with the meaning of 'I', we get a reflexive identifying condition with u as a constituent:

> being the speaker of **u**

I also call this level of content 'content$_M$' because it is the content we assign to the utterance based only on the Meaning of the indexical used. That is, although we have the utterance itself, we haven't taken account of its context.

On the reflexive-referential theory, as we have developed it so far, then, a term has indexical content or content$_M$. Plausible meanings for some familiar indexicals, in line with our discussion of chapter 2:

> If u is an utterance of 'I', the indexical content of u is the identifying condition, *being the speaker of* **u**.

> If u is an utterance of 'you', the indexical content of u is the identifying condition, *being the addressee of* **u**.

If u is an utterance of 'now', the basic content of u is the identifying condition, *being the relevant time of* **u**,

If u is an utterance of 'that ϕ', the basic content of u is the identifying condition, *being the salient ϕ to which the speaker of* **u** *directs attention.*

What about statements (utterances of declarative sentences)? We saw above how Reichenbach analyzed Luther's utterance at Worms; he called it θ, but I'll just give it a number:

(22) $st[(\iota x)(Ez)sp(x, (22), z), (\iota z)(Ex)sp(x, (22), z)]$

In our language, Reichenbach identifies proposition (P^x22) as the content of (22):

(P^x22)   *The speaker of* **(22)** stands at *the location of* **(22)**

We have here a general proposition about two identifying conditions, *the speaker of* **(22)** and *the place of* **(22)**. Each of these is a singular condition, with (22) as a constituent. In the terminology of chapter 2, (P^x22) is a lumpy general proposition, that is covertly about the utterance (22).

This proposition fits Burks's description of aspect (iv) (see section 3.2), which results from combining the meaning of an expression with the token or utterance of it. On the reflexive-referential account, the meaning of a sentence like Luther's is a condition on utterances, and Reichenbach's analysis fills the parameter of that condition with the utterance itself. It seems that Reichenbach's proposition or something like it deserves a central place in our account. And so it does. On the reflexive-referential account, this proposition is the content$_M$ of the utterance.

5.3   Indexical content and referential content

Now we can add indexical content to our simple semantics. The double line indicates the passage from *reflexive* to *incremental* content. That is, the content above the double line is a proposition about the utterance, while the contents below the line get at what *else* has to be true about the world, *given* the facts about the utterance.

In Table 3 parentheses indicate possibility. Thus while indexicals are always associated with utterance reflexive identifying conditions at the level of indexical content, descriptions may or may not be, depending on whether they incorporate indexicals.

Let's look for a moment at the third level of Table 3, referential content. This is unchanged from our vanilla theory, except for addition of the cell for indexicals. In accordance with referentialist arguments, we take the referential content of the utterance of an indexical to an individual, time or place.

Now consider an utterance of the description

(23)   The house you live in

directed at Burks. At the level of indexical content, (23) is associated with an utterance reflexive identifying condition:

$(C^x 23)$ being the house *the addressee of* **(23)** lives in.

The condition $(C^x 23)$ is reflexive because the utterance (23) itself is a constituent of a constituent of the identifying condition, and so a covert constituent of $(C^x 23)$.

If we load the description in (23) with the fact that Burks is the addressee we have:

$(C^r 23)$ being the house **Burks** lives in

$(C^r 23)$ is manifestly about Burks, rather than covertly about the utterance directed at him.

Now consider the whole utterance,

(24)   The house you live in is quite attractive.

The indexical content of (24) is a proposition that is covertly about the utterance:

$(P^x 24)$ That *the house the addressee of* **(24)** *lives in* is quite attractive

The referential content of (24), loaded with the fact that Burks is the speaker of (24), is a general proposition that is covertly about Burks:

$(P24)$ That *the house* **Burks** *lives in* is quite attractive

TABLE 3: VANILLA SEMANTICS INCORPORATING INDEXICAL CONTENT

	If α is a name	If α is an indexical	If α is a description	If α is an n-place predicate	If α is a sentence
the Meaning of α is	a rule associating an individual with α	a rule associating an u-reflexive identifying condition with α	a rule associating an (u-reflexive) identifying condition with α	a rule associating an (u-reflexive) n-ary condition on individuals with α	a rule associating an (u-reflexive) proposition with α
the Indexical Content of an utterance of α is	an individual	an u-reflexive identifying condition	an (u-reflexive) identifying condition	an (u-reflexive) n-ary condition on individuals	an (u-reflexive) proposition
the Referential Content of an utterance of α is	an individual	an individual	an identifying condition	an n-ary condition on individuals	a proposition
the Designational Content of an utterance of α is	an individual	an individual	an individual	an n-ary condition on individuals	a proposition
the Extension of an utterance of α is	an Individual	an Individual	an Individual	an n-tuple	a truth-value

5.4   Varieties of content

The objects we find in level 2 of Table 3, the indexical contents, seem to be coherently described, metaphysically benign
objects. But do they deserve to be called *contents*? Should indexical content fit into an account of meaning? Don't the referentialist
arguments simply show that it is not content, and should not be
called content?

Consider (P^x22), the indexical content of Luther's remark.
(P^x22) is clearly not what Luther said, as the same-saying and
counterfactual arguments establish. He didn't say anything about
his own utterance, and he referred to himself with 'I', rather
than describing himself. So (P^x22) is not a good candidate for the
official content of Luther's remark. But isn't that what we mean
by 'the content of an utterance.' How can there be two kinds of
content?

Varieties of truth-conditions

A problem that underlies the simple picture of meaning and content is now going to come to the surface. We introduced content
in chapter 1 in terms of truth-conditions. The content of an utterance is a proposition that incorporates its truth-conditions. The
problem is that the concept of 'truth-conditions of an utterance' is
a *relative concept*, although it is often treated as if it were absolute.
Instead of thinking in terms of *the* truth-conditions of an utterance, we should think of the truth conditions of an utterance *given*
various facts about it. And when we do this we are led to see that
talking about *the* content of an utterance is an oversimplification.

Suppose that you are at an international philosophy meeting.
During what seems a stupid lecture, the person next to you
writes a note which he passes to you. It says, "Cet homme est
brillant." He then whispers, in English, "Don't you agree?" You
are a confirmed monolingual; at first you don't even recognize the
language in which the message is written. To avoid compounding
ignorance with impertinence, you nod. All you can infer about
the message is that it is a statement—an utterance, with which

one could agree or disagree. Do you know the truth-conditions of his message?

Given the ordinary philosophical concept of the truth-conditions of an utterance, you certainly do not. You have no idea what proposition is expressed. If you did, you wouldn't have nodded as if you agreed.

But you could list some conditions, such that, were they met, the message would be true. Call the message **m**; **m** is true if there is a proposition P, such that in the language in which **m** was written, its words have a certain meaning, and in the context in which **m** was written, words with that meaning express P, and P is true.

It is fair to call these truth-conditions of **m**, because they are conditions such that, were they satisfied, **m** would be true. They are not, however, what philosophers usually have in mind when they talk about the truth-conditions or content of the message. They would have in mind the proposition that a certain person, the lecturer, was brilliant. These truth-conditions are reflexive, conditions on **m** *itself*. Traditional truth-conditions are *incremental*; they are conditions on the *subject matter*; the are what *else* has to be true, given the linguistic and contextual facts about the utterance.

The philosophical concept of truth-conditions is a special case of a more general one: the truth-conditions of an utterance *given* certain facts about it. In the example, what you know about **m** is its truth-conditions given only the barest facts about it, that it is a statement. You can specify conditions under which **m** would be true, but because you know so little about **m** itself, those conditions have a lot to do with **m**'s relation to the rest of the world and say little about the world independently of **m**. The familiar philosophical concept of truth-conditions corresponds to the case in which one knows a lot about **m**; in this case the conditions will pertain to the world outside **m**, not **m** itself.

If your high-school French started to return to you, you might reason as follows:

> *Given* that the language of **m** is French, and *given* the meaning of 'Cet homme est brillant' in French, and *given* the fact that the author of **m** intended to use the words 'Cet homme' to refer to a that person (looking at the lecturer), **m** is true iff *that person is brilliant.*

As you figure out more about **m**, fixing more of its linguistic properties, the conditions that had to be fulfilled for its truth become more focussed on the world. The *additional* or *incremental* conditions required for the truth of **m**, given all that you figured out about **m**, were conditions on a certain person, that he be brilliant. Our philosophical concept of truth-conditions of an utterance is the *incremental* conditions required for truth, given that all of these linguistic factors are fixed.

This picture of truth-conditions as relative is simply a matter of treating them like other conditions we ask about. Whenever we ask about the conditions under which something has a certain property, we take certain facts as given. What we want to know is *what else*, what additional facts, have to obtain, for the thing to have that property, *given* the facts we assume. I ask you "Under what conditions will Clinton get re-elected?" and you say, "He has to carry California." You are taking for granted a number of things—that he will lose the South, do well in the in the Northeast, get at least two midwestern states. *Given all of this*, what *else* does he need? To carry California.

Usually, the conditions for x to be such and such will be conditions *on* x. But not always. This conversation makes sense:

Under what conditions will Clinton win?

A high proportion of Democrats must vote.

Here the respondent doesn't tell us what Clinton has to be like or what Clinton has to do to win. He takes the relevant facts about Clinton as given and fixed, and says what the rest of the world has to be like for Clinton to win.

It's the same with the usual concept of truth-conditions. What does the world have to be like for **m** to be true? That guy must be a brilliant lecturer. Right—*given* the facts about the language, the words, the meaning and the context of **m**, that's what *else* is needed.

As I mentioned above, I use three different kinds of content in the account of indexicals. These correspond to three kinds of facts one might take as fixed in assessing truth-conditions:

> The indexical content or *content*$_M$ of an utterance corresponds to the truth-conditions of the utterance given the facts that fix the language of the utterance, the words involved, their syntax and their *meaning*.[24]

> The referential content or *content*$_C$ of an utterance corresponds to the truth-conditions given all of these factors, plus the facts about the *context* of the utterance that are needed to fix the designation of indexicals.

> The designational content or *content*$_D$ of an utterance corresponds to the truth-conditions given all of these factors, plus the additional facts that are needed to fix the *designation* of the terms that remain (definite descriptions in particular, but also possessives, etc.).

Consider:

(25)   You were born in the capital of Nebraska.

The reader will quickly grasp that the language is English; the identity of the words is clear, the syntax is unproblematic and there are no relevant ambiguities. So what the reader grasps is just what our first concept fixes. What the reader understands is the content$_M$; he will grasp that the truth of (25) requires:

(P^{x}25)   That *the addressee of* **(25)** was born in *the capital of* **Nebraska**.

If I now add the relevant contextual fact, that the speaker of (25) was addressing my son Jim, the reader will grasp the content$_C$:

---

[24]Note that, given our assumption that names name rather than denote, this means that the designata of names is fixed at the level of *content*$_M$.

(P^{r}25)   **Jim** was born in *the capital of* **Nebraska**.

The reader no doubt knows that Lincoln is the capital of Nebraska. Hence she also grasps the content$_D$ of (25):

Jim was born in **the capital of Nebraska**.

which is the same as:

(P^{r}7)   **Jim** was born in **Lincoln**.

5.5 Official content

Indexical content is a useful tool for understanding the motivation and impact of utterances. But it is not our ordinary concept of content. It is not what I have called official content, the content that corresponds to what the speaker says. As we saw in chapter 1, there are two main arguments for this. I want to return to those arguments now for two reasons. First I want to point out that we can accept the arguments, as long as we don't take them to show more than they do, without in any way giving up the idea that indexical content is cognitively relevant.

Recall that I use 'Official Content' to get at the concept of content built our ordinary concepts of 'what is said' and 'says the same thing'. I think the referentialist arguments show that official content is referential content, but in no way show that that is the only sort of content.[25]

Second, we need to sort out the difference between referential content and Burks's slightly different concept, aspect (v) of 3.2, the 'information conveyed' by an utterance.

Consider my utterance, directed at my son Jim:

(26)   You were born in Lincoln.

The content$_M$ of (26) is a proposition about (26). But we would ordinarily count me as having said the same thing to him as he said to me with his utterance

---

[25]I explore weakening this agreement a bit below in chapter 8; the referentialist arguments show only that for a wide variety of cases referential content is the *default* official content.

(27)   I was born in Lincoln.

and the same thing I say to a third party with my utterance

(7)   Jim was born in Lincoln

But these two utterances have quite different contents$_M$ than (26) has. The content$_M$ of (26) is a proposition about (26) itself, while the content$_M$ of (7) is just a singular proposition about Jim (since names name, their designation is fixed by their meaning). It seems then that it is the individual designated by the subutterance of 'you', and not the condition of being the addressee of that subutterance, that makes it into the official content of (26).

To understand the counterfactual circumstances argument, we need to keep clearly in mind the difference between the conditions under which an utterance is true, and conditions under which *what is said by the utterance* (or perhaps better, *what the speaker says*, in virtue of making the utterance) is true. We can separate these, by considering counterfactual circumstances in which the utterance is false, but what is said by the utterance is true (Kaplan, 1989a).

Suppose, contrary to fact, that when I uttered (26) I was mistaken, and was talking to my son Joe rather than Jim. In those circumstances, my utterance would have been false, since Joe was born in California. And what I would have said in those circumstances, that Joe was born in Lincoln, is false. But what I *actually* said, since I actually was talking to Jim, was that he was born in Lincoln. And that proposition, that Jim was born in Lincoln, would have been true, even if, when I uttered (26), I was talking to Joe.

The upshot of these arguments is that the official content of (26) is a singular proposition about Jim. This is the same proposition that Jim expressed with (27), and that I expressed with (7). And it is a proposition that would still be true even if I were talking to Joe rather than Jim, although of course then I would not have expressed it with (26), but a quite different and false proposition about Joe.

Our other two kinds of content, referential content and designational content, both assign this proposition to (26), (27) and (7). But these differ from,

(8)   The manager of Kinko's was born in the capital of Nebraska.

The referential content of (8) is not a singular proposition about Jim.

Designational content—Content$_D$—corresponds to truth-conditions with *all* the facts that determine designation of terms fixed, including in this case the fact that Jim is the manager of Kinko's. So the designational content of (8) is our singular proposition about Jim, the same proposition that is the referential content of (7).

Designational content corresponds to Burks's concept of 'information conveyed'. To introduce his concept of information, Burks uses the following two utterances:

(28)   'This book is red' uttered by a speaker pointing at a certain book, located at coordinates x, y, z, t

(29)   'The book at coordinates x, y, z, t is red'

Using 'refer' as I use 'designate', Burks says,

> ... though these sentences do differ in meaning, in one sense of 'information' they both convey the same information, for they both refer to the same object and predicate the same property of it. We can say, then, that [(28)] is a substitute for [(29)] in the sense that it conveys the same information; but it is not an exact substitute for [(29)] in the sense that it differs in indexical- and symbolic-meaning ....

On this concept (7) – (9), (26) and (27) all convey the same information. Which corresponds to official content, referential content or content$_D$? It depends on whether we think of definite descriptions as referring or describing. If they refer, then they contribute the objects they designate to official content, and the right answer is that content$_D$ is official content. If they describe, then referential content is the right answer. For the purposes of this essay, I have accepted the traditional account of definite descriptions as describing.[26]

With this understanding of definite descriptions, it is referential content that corresponds to official content. When we compare what people say, and consider the counterfactual circumstances in which what they say is true, we fix the meaning and context, but let other facts vary, even the ones that fix the designation of definite descriptions. Consider,

(25)   You were born in the capital of Nebraska

said to Jim. When we think of the possible worlds in which this is true, what do we require of them? We don't fix the facts about which thing descriptions designate before considering the worlds. So worlds in which Jim was born in Omaha, and Omaha is the capital of Nebraska do get in. But we do fix the contextual facts, and so the designation of indexicals, before we consider the worlds. So worlds in which Jim was born in Iowa don't get in, even if in those worlds I am talking to Marlon, and Marlon was born in Nebraska. And we fix the meaning before considering worlds. So worlds in which Jim was born in Wyoming don't get in, even if in them 'You were born in the capital of Nebraska' means that $2 + 2 = 4$.

5.6 Stretching cognitive content

The meaning of an indexical or sentence containing indexicals provides a condition directly or covertly about utterances. We

---

[26] As noted above, I am ignoring Donnellan's distinction between attributive and referential uses of definite descriptions for the time being. This is not to imply that there is anything absurd about the idea that definite descriptions refer. Recanati has a clear conception of this. He sees terms as having or lacking a certain feature, 'ref'. In my terms, a term that has this feature contributes the object it designates to official content, whether the term names or denotes. Names and indexicals have this feature in virtue of their meaning. On Recanati's view definite descriptions do not have this feature built into their meaning, but it can be added at a pragmatic level in particular cases (1993). One can surmise that David Kaplan's 'dthat' operator is a way of making the 'ref' feature syntactically explicit; 'dthat' itself is, of course, open to various interpretations, even by its inventor (1989).

move from this condition to the indexical content of an utterance of that type by filling the parameter of that condition with the utterance itself. So, in the example we just considered, the content$_M$ of (25) is a proposition covertly about (25) itself:

(P^{x}25): That *The addressee of* **(25)** was born in *the capital of* **Nebraska**.

As we noted, (P^{x}25) certainly does not seem to be the official content of (25), what the speaker said when he uttered (25). It is rather the indexical content. It is this level of content that we must use to understand the cognitive significance of statements — the interaction between semantics and thought — in examples involving indexicals and demonstratives.

Let's return to Stretch, the long dog that seems to be pictured on the cover. (Readers of the cloth edition please refer to the last page in the book.)

If I were to point first at Stretch's head and then at Stretch's tail and say,

(30)   That dog is that dog

I would have said something informative, something that, assuming my credibility, would clear up the question of how many dogs there were on the veranda of the Bookstore. If I had said exactly the same thing, while pointing twice to Stretch's head, I would not have conveyed any information, but said something quite trivial, and would not have cleared up the question at all. (I'll call these two possibilities for (30) *versions*. The versions differ just in whether the demonstrations are different, the first to the head and the second to the tail, or both just to the head.)

If on the other hand I had said,

(31)   That dog is not that dog

pointing first to the head and then to the tail, I would have said something that answered the question of how many dogs there were on the veranda, but answered it wrongly; I would have said something false, but, it seems, something that might have been true. On the other hand, if I had said (31) while pointing twice to Stretch's head—the second version of (31)— I would have said something quite absurd.

Let's call the two utterances of 'that dog' u_1 and u_2. So in the first versions of (30) and (31) u_1 is to Stretch's head and u_2 to his tail, in the second versions, both are to Stetch's head.

TABLE 4: STRETCH THE DOG
CONTENTS OF UTTERANCES u_1 AND u_2
OF 'THAT DOG' IN (30) AND (31)

	u_1	u_2
Indexical Content or Content$_M$	the dog that the speaker of u_1 is attending to	the dog that the speaker of u_2 is attending to
Referential Content or Content$_C$	Stretch	Stretch
Designational Content	Stretch	Stretch

The only place we find a difference in the content is at the level of indexical content (See Table 4). But this difference is enough to explain the difference in cognitive significance.

The question of how many dogs there are on the veranda comes down to the question of whether the dog's head that the speaker and the listener see and the dog's tail that the speaker and the listener see belong to the same dog. Nobody really cares about whether the the speaker is attending to the same dogs when he utters u_1 and u_2. When the question is raised, the speaker hasn't said anything, u_1 and u_2 don't even exist, so one could hardly worry about them. The photograph on the cover give us a picture of the puzzling situation, and the utterances u_1 and u_2 are not in the picture at all. So what can the indexical content of (30) have to do with the question raised about dogs on the veranda?

The relevance is simply that *given* the facts about where the speaker of u_1 or u_2 is directing attention—the facts conveyed by demonstrations, or made apparent by eye-gaze—the truth of the indexical content of utterance (30), with demonstrations first to the head and then to the tail, will entail that there is only a single dog on the veranda. The purpose of the different demonstrations is to create two different cognitive paths. The demonstrations serve to start the paths off in different directions, to associate them with different perceptions on the hearer's part, the perceptions of the head and of the tail. *The indexical content is not what is said, nor is it what the speaker intends to convey, nor is it the information that answers the hearer's inquiry about how many dogs there are.* But the indexical content, *given* what is common knowledge between the speaker and listener, that the speaker directs attention first to the dog's head and then to the dog's tail, implies that which the speaker wishes to convey, that a single dog has both *that* head and *that* tail.

On the other hand, if the speaker says (31) with different demonstrations, he will convey something false, that there is not a dog with the seen head and seen tail. If he says (31) with two demonstrations to the head, he will have said something quite absurd.

In the first case, in which (31) is uttered with different demonstrations, there is a possible way for the utterances to be true—a fairly plausible possibility. In the world in which there are two dogs, one with a head we can see and one with a tail we can see, this utterance of (31) would be true. This is not to say there is a world in which Stretch is two dogs. In going from world to world what we are 'taking with us' is not Stretch, but the utterance.

In contrast, it is not at all easy to find a world in which the utterance of (31) with two demonstrations to the dog's head comes out true. I do not say it is impossible; the utterance of (31) takes time, and there are no doubt possible worlds in which dogs can be switched quicker than the eyes can notice. But this is a lot less likely than there being two dogs.

It seems then that given the perspective developed here, there is no problem with the different versions of (30) and (31) being used to convey quite different information. The difference in demonstrations leads to a difference in truth-conditions between the two versions of (30) (or (31)), even though on the Stretch hypothesis they are demonstrations of the same dog, the utterances of 'that dog' are references to the same dog, and the meanings of both utterances are the same.

Given these two different beginnings, we can get two quite different cognitive paths in the first versions of (30) and (31):

> For u_1: The dog the utterer of u_1 directs the hearer's attention to; the dog that fellow directs my attention to; the dog that fellow is pointing at/gazing at; the dog with that head; that$_p$ dog.

> For u_2: The dog the utterer of u_2 directs the hearer's attention to; the dog that fellow directs my attention to; the dog that fellow is pointing at/gazing at; the dog with that tail; that$_{p'}$ dog.

> Where p is the hearer's perception of Stretch's head, and p' the perception of Stretch's tail.

This example highlights some of the difficulties with what we might call the *naive referentialist* theory of content, the view that official content is all we have to work with. (I'll sometimes call the reflexive-referential theory *critical referentialism* in contrast). Consider the first case of (30), with successive demonstrations via head and tail. The referential content, given the relevant contextual facts, is simply the proposition that Stretch is Stretch. This is, according to the rigid referentialist theory, what is said by my utterance. This is, as we have seen, compatible with allowing that I convey, and intend to convey, quite different information, namely, the proposition that there is but a single dog on the Bookstore veranda. But it seems in this case that that is not enough. It seems odd to say that I said that Stretch was Stretch at all.

Companion to the naive referentialist account of content, is the naive referentialist account of possibility. The possibilities up for grabs, on this account, are those in which Stretch is Stretch (for either utterance of (30)) or those in which Stretch is not Stretch (for either utterance of (31)). On this view we have some kind of necessity for (30), since every world with Stretch is a world in which Stretch is Stretch, and some kind of impossibility for (31), since no world with Stretch has Stretch not identical with himself. But these do not seem to be the possibilities that are at issue at all. The possibilities which I seem to rule out with (30), and deem actual with (31), are the quite legitimate ones where there are two dogs on the veranda. The contingency involved is not that of one dog being two, but that of two dog-perceptions that are actually of the same dog being of two different dogs. This is a possibility or conceivability that comes out at the level of reflexive content, but not at the referential or subject matter content.[27]

5.7 Austin's two tubes

In *What's the Meaning of 'This'* (1990) David Austin develops a very focused problem for the referentialist, the *two tubes* case. The two tubes are part of an experiment to test Smith's ability to focus his eyes independently. The situation is rather complicated, so I'll quote extensively from Austin:

> The experimental apparatus consists of a large opaque screen with two small eye holes in it. Two tubes lead from the eye holes and can be oriented in a large number of directions ... Smith is to look through the tubes simultaneously and to report what he sees as he focuses his eyes independently. . . .[he] knows that he does not know how the tubes are oriented. . .What he sees through his right eye is a circular red spot, which he dubs 'this;' what he sees through his left eye is a precisely similar circular red spot, which he dubs 'that.' Because Smith is focusing his eyes independently, he does not have one, unified visual field. . .he has two, independent visual fields and at the center of each he sees a red spot. He thinks to himself,
>
> ... this is red and that is red
>
> A somewhat pedantic and cautious person, he also thinks to himself,

---

[27] In *Knowledge, Possibility and Consciousness* (2001) I argue that confusions over the contents of our thoughts about what is possible are a the root of the modal argument against physicalism.

... this = this and that = that

... Smith wonders, "Is this = that?" ... Smith's interior mono-logue goes like this:

I know that I know that this is red and that this = this and that that is red and that that = that, and I know that I do not believe that this = that or that this ≠ that, and I know that I do not disbelieve that this = that or that this ≠ that.

And about all of this Smith is entirely correct; his interior monologue expresses nothing but truths.

Finally, suppose that the tubes are in fact pointed at the very same red spot. (20-21)

Given all of this, Austin sees a problem for the referentialist. Consider the following, which are from Austin except for a bit of terminology. (We'll call the dot Smith sees twice over 'Dot'.)

(A)   It is possible that a believer believe a singular propo-sition with a contingent thing other than himself as a constituent.

(B)   If (A) is true, then Smith believes the singular propo-sition he expresses by 'this = this' and the singular proposition he expresses by 'that = that'.

(6)   By 'this = this' Smith expresses the proposition that **Dot = Dot**.

(7)   By 'that = that' Smith expresses the proposition that **Dot = Dot**.

(8)   By 'this = that' Smith expresses the proposition that **Dot = Dot**.

(C)   If Smith believes the singular proposition he expresses by 'this = this' and the singular proposition he expresses by 'that = that,' then he believes the singular proposition he expresses by 'this = that'.

(D)   It is not the case that Smith believes the singular propo-
        sition he expresses by 'this = that'.

Austin takes the referentialist to be committed to everything
through (C), and thinks that (D) is obvious from common sense
applied to the situation:

> After all, Smith wonders, "Is this = that?" So it seems that (D)
> must be true if Smith's ignorance is to be accounted for. The
> trouble for the advocate of [singular] propositions is that, on
> that view, all of (A), (B), (C) and (D) are true. But they are also
> inconsistent and so can't all be true.(23)

What does the reflexive-referential theory say about this? First
let's look at the sentences

(32)   this = this

(33)   that = that

(34)   this = that

None of the statements is really trivial simply in virtue of its
meaning; this comes out clearly at the level of reflexive content:

(P^x32)   The object the speaker of **the first use of 'this' in (32)**
            attends to as he speaks it = the object the speaker of **the
            second use of 'this' in (32)** attends to as he speaks it.

(P^x33)   The object the speaker of **the first use of 'that' in (33)**
            attends to as he speaks it = the object the speaker of **the
            second use of 'that' in (33)** attends to as he speaks it.

(P^x34)   The object the speaker of **the use of 'this' in (34)** attends
            to as he speaks it = the object the speaker of **the use of
            'that' in (34)** attends to as he speaks it.

In this circumstance, with the background filled in by Austin, we
know that the same speaker and the same perceptual buffer are
involved in the two uses of 'this' in (32) and the two uses of 'that'
in (33), and that different buffers are involved in the uses of 'this'
and 'that' in (34). Even though the three statements express the

same proposition given Smith's situation, they do not have the same reflexive truth-conditions.

What about the beliefs? Let's let's call the perceptual buffer receiving input from that right eye 'r' and that from the left eye 'l'. Then the reflexive contents of Smith's two beliefs are:

(P^{x}32b)   That **r** and **r** are of the same object;

(P^{x}33b)   That l and l are of the same object;

If Smith had a belief that (34) expressed, its reflexive content would be:

(P^{x}34b)   That **r** and l are of the same object;

Connected reflexive content

Notice that the reflexive contents of the beliefs are *not* the same as the reflexive contents of the statements that express them — given the reflexive nature of the contents, they could not be. The relation between the contents is what I call 'architectural' following Israel and Perry (1991). The architectural truth-conditions of a representation[28] take as given important connections to some other representation, but not the further connections to designata. There is a causal connection between the buffer **r** and the uses of the referential expression 'this' in the statements (32) and (34) and between the buffer l and the uses of 'that' in (33) and (34). The buffers *govern* the utterances. The material that is predicatively associated with the uses of 'this' depends on the ideas that are associated with the buffer **r**. This architectural connection gives rise to a new kind of content: the content *given* the architectural connections. For example,

> *Given* that **r** governs the use of 'this' in (34) and that l governs the use of 'that' in (34), (34) is true iff **r** and l are of the same object.

---

[28]Or, more generally, a signal, that is, any state or event considered with respect to what it shows about the rest of the world, given various constraints and facts.

Hence the content of statement (32), given the architectural connections of its referring expressions, is (P^x32b). The content of statement (33), given the architectural connections of its referring expressions, is (P^x33b). If Smith had a belief that (34) expressed, its reflexive content would be (P^x34b). In general,

> If statement expresses a belief, the content of the statement, given its architectural connections to the belief, will be the same as the reflexive content of the belief.

We'll call this kind of content the *connected reflexive content* of a statement.

With this in mind, let's return to Smith's internal monologue, simplified somewhat so we can ignore issues about the relation between knowledge and belief, and issues about iterated attitude reports:

> I believe that this is red and that this = this and that that is red and that that = that, and I do not believe that this = that or that this ≠ that, and I do not disbelieve that this = that or that this ≠ that.

Each of the statements Smith makes to himself says something about those of his beliefs which involve the perceptual buffers **r** and **l**. When he says that he believes that 'this is red and that this = this', what he says is true if and only if he has a belief with the connected reflexive content of his statement, that **r** is of a red spot, and that **r** is of the same spot it is of. When he says that does not believe that 'this = that', what he says is true if and only if he does not have a belief with the connected reflexive content of his statement, that **r** is of the same spot as **l**. When he says he does not disbelieve that 'this = that' what he says is true if he does not have a belief that contradicts the connected reflexive content of 'this = that', that is, a belief whose reflexive content is that **r** and **l** are not of the same spot.

What we believe, and how we report it

Thus, given the concepts of the reflexive content of beliefs and statements, and the architectural content of a statement given its connections to the beliefs that motivate it, we can sort out what is going on in the two tubes puzzle. This is not the same as providing a semantics for belief reports. I am not going to attempt to provide such a semantics in this book, but I will briefly explain how I see the reflexive-referential theory fitting into the account developed in 'The Prince and the Phonebooth' and Crimmins's *Talk About Beliefs* (1992).

On a 'semantically innocent' approach to statements like

(35)   Smith believes that Harold is a spy

one has to provide truth conditions using the semantic value one's theory provides for 'Harold is a spy'. 'Semantic innocence' means that one does not introduce new semantic values for sentences that are embedded in such attitude reports. So the referentialist seems to have Smith, the relation of belief, the singular proposition that **Harold** is a spy, and the apparatus of logic with which to work. If one believes in beliefs, the most straightforward approach is to suppose that (35) is true if and only if Smith has a belief whose (referential) content is that singular proposition. On this view, Smith's report to himself in the experimental situation,

(36)   I do not believe this = that

turns out to be false. That referential content of the statement that is embedded in this report is simply that **Dot** = **Dot**, and he has two beliefs with that content, the one he thinks to himself as 'this = this' and the one he thinks to himself as 'that = that'. One approach, taken by Scott Soames and Nathan Salmon,[29] is to say that this result is correct. This is sometimes called the 'bite the bullet' approach, since it requires accepting that many prima facie true belief-reports are false (like this one) and many prima facie false reports are true. One example: the report that Clinton's boyhood friend of chapter 1 believes that Bill Clinton was Bill Blythe. Soames and Salmon make considerable progress

---

[29]See Soames, 1989, Salmon, 1986. Barwise and I also adopted this approach in Barwise and Perry, 1983.

in convincing us that these prima facie intuitions can be explained away pragmatically.

Those who are unconvinced must come up with something else. In 'The Prince and the Phonebooth', Mark Crimmins and I proposed that belief-reports express propositions that have the notions involved in the beliefs as unarticulated constituents. Applied to (36), we would say that Smith is right, because he doesn't have a belief *involving the buffers* **r** *and* **l** whose content is that **Dot** = **Dot**. Applied to the Clinton-Blythe case, we would say that the boyhood friend did not believe that Clinton was Blythe, because he didn't have a belief with the content **Clinton** = **Clinton** *involving his Clinton and Blythe buffers*. Suppose we give Smith a break from his experimental labors and take him to the Stanford Bookstore, where he sees Stretch. He says, pointing first at Stretch's tail and then at his head, "I do not believe that this dog is that dog." We'd take his statement to be true, with the perceptual buffers connected to his utterances of 'this dog' and 'that dog' as unarticulated constituents of his self-report.

Then I point to Stretch's tail and head too, while I tell you:

(37)   Smith does not believe that this dog is that dog.

Crimmins and I want this report to have Smith's perceptual buffers as unarticulated constituents. The relevant buffers are not causally connected to the utterances in a very direct way, since it is Smith's buffers that we need but we need them to be constituents of my report. The step from my use of 'this dog' and 'that dog' to Smith's buffers is pragmatic; you are to pick up that I am talking about those of Smith's beliefs that are connected to perceptual buffers he had while in a situation similar to the one I am in, and am putting you in, with my demonstrations, first focusing on Stretch's head, and then on his behind.

It really seems more plausible at this point to suppose that what I am calling to your attention are certain *types* of notions: the type of notions that one has when looking at Stretch's head, and the type one has when one focuses on his behind. Where T_{head} and T_{tail} are the types, my statement (37) is true iff Smith does not have a belief involving notions, the first of type T_{head} and the second of type T_{tail}, and the content that **Stretch** is **Stretch**. The retreat to types of notions also gives us more flexibility in treating cases in which the reporter is mistaken about whether the believer has a notion at all, and reports about the beliefs of more than one person. This theory is developed and defended by Crimmins in *Talk About Beliefs*. It has not found unanimous acceptance, and a number of criticisms and alternatives would need to be considered in a full discussion, which I won't provide here. We can see, however, that the reflexive-referential theory fits well with this account of belief-reports.

6

Names and the Co-reference Problem

6.1 Introduction

As we noted in chapter 1, the reflexive-referential solution to the problem of co-reference for indexicals does not carry over in any obvious way to the case of proper names, unless one thinks that proper names are indexicals. I do not think that proper names are indexicals, and yet I claim that the solution does generalize. The reason is that it is not indexicality that is at the bottom of our solution, but reflexivity. In this chapter we'll look at the cases of Ernst Mach and David Israel which both require us to understand the difference between names, indexicals and demonstratives. We'll start with the Israel case, take a break to begin developing an account of names, and then return to Mach. Then we'll look at Kripke's Paderewski case (Kripke, 1979), which involves only proper names, and only one of them!

6.2 The computer scientist

The reader will recall this example from chapter 1:

(4)   "I am a computer scientist." (said by David Israel)

(5)   "David is a computer scientist." (said by someone who is referring to David Israel with 'David')

Consider two cases. In Case 1 Israel is talking to a guest lecturer who doesn't know him at a CSLI colloquium. Israel wants to reassure the guest lecturer that he knows something about computer languages. It is natural for him to use (4) to achieve this goal;

(5) wouldn't work. In Case 2, Israel is being asked questions by a government bureaucrat about SRI employees, including David. David feels obliged to answer truthfully the question 'Is David Israel now or has he ever been a computer scientist?' But he does not want to disclose that he himself is a computer scientist. To do so, he fears, would subject him to sarcastic comments from the bureaucrat, who clearly thinks that all computer scientists are nerdy and unkempt. He can achieve this by uttering (5) but not by uttering (4). Hence utterances (4) and (5) could be motivated by different beliefs and desires on the part of the speaker, and might give rise to different beliefs on the part of the listener.

At the beginning of this essay, this seemed hard to explain on the referentialist account, according to which (4) and (5) have the same content, the singular proposition that David Israel is a computer scientist:

(P^{r}5)   **David Israel** is a computer scientist.

We can now see our way clear to solving part of the problem. Any competent English speaker will grasp the indexical content of (4) (recall that ι is the utterance of 'I'):

(P^{x}4)   That *the speaker of* ι is a computer scientist.

(P^{x}4) is not the proposition expressed by (4); as we saw, that is (P^{r}5). But I have argued that this does not mean that (P^{x}4) is irrelevant to the cognitive significance of (4).

In Case 1, Israel wanted the hearer to recognize that the person spoken about was also the person speaking. The plan of understanding that he has in mind goes roughly like this:

> The hearer will perceive my utterance, and, as a competent speaker of English will recognize that it is true iff the person who makes it is a computer scientist (P^{x}4). He will also see that I —the person in front of him and talking to him— am the speaker of the utterance. So he will learn that the person in front of him is a computer scientist, and will realize he can learn more about this fascinating field by asking questions of this person and listening attentively to the answers.

In Case 2, when Israel does not want the hearer to recognize that he is speaking to a computer scientist, he does not refer to himself with the expression 'I', and so does not disclose to the hearer that the person with whom he is talking is a computer scientist. So we have an explanation of why David chose to utter (4) in Case 1 but not in Case 2.[30]

Still, we have only solved part of our problem. In Case 2, David does want his hearer to realize that the person designated by 'David Israel' on his list of SRI employees is a computer scientist. He manages to bring this impact about by using his own name when he responds. How does this work?

6.3 Names and conventions

Let's review the distinctions and terminology about designation that we have used.

> Terms *refer* if they contribute the object they designate, rather than an identifying condition, to official content, so that their official contents are singular propositions about the object designated.

> Terms *describe* if they contribute an identifying condition to official content.

> Terms *denote* if the conventions of language associate them with modes of presentation, that is, with conditions an object is required to meet to be the one that is designated.

> Terms *name*, on the other hand, if the conventions that secure designations for them associate them with objects, rather than conditions on objects.

---

[30]See Taylor's discussion of Smith, the risk-loving murderer who volunteers as a witness for Detective Jones and tells her all about the murderer, Smith. Smith is risk-loving but not a complete idiot, and so he uses the third-person (Taylor, 1993).

We agreed at the outset on the assumption that descriptions describe; we've accepted the classical referentialist arguments that indexicals and names refer. Descriptions clearly denote and I've argued that indexicals do too. That leaves the question whether names denote or name. My terminology allows me to state my account of names in a way that sounds persuasively trivial: names name. That is:

TABLE 5: VARIETIES OF DESIGNATION

	Refer	Describe
Name	Proper names	
Denote	Indexicals	Descriptions

When a person or thing is assigned a name, a *permissive convention* is established: that name *may* be used to designate that person. When David Israel's parents named him 'David', they established a convention that made it possible for people to designate their son with the name 'David'. It did not preclude people from using 'David' to designate other people, or using other means of designating David.

When a name is used in a conversation or text to refer to a given person, the speaker is exploiting a convention of this sort. A single name like 'David' may be associated with hundreds of thousands of people by different permissive conventions. In the abstract, the problem of knowing which conventions are being exploited when one apprehends a token containing the word 'David' are considerable. And when one sees something like 'David was here' scrawled on a wall one may be completely clueless as to which of the millions of Davids is being designated. But usually various factors work to make the use of proper names a practical way of talking about things. I only know a small minority of the Davids that can be designated with 'David'; the ones I know overlap in various fairly predictable ways with the ones known by people I regularly meet in various contexts; principles of charity dictate that I take my interlocutors to be designating Davids that might have, or might be taken to have, the properties that are being predicated of the David in question;

and I can always just ask.

The role of context in resolving the issues of which naming conventions are being exploited is quite different from its role with indexicals. In the case of indexicals, the meaning of a given expression determines that certain more or less specific contextual relationships to the utterance and utterer—who is speaking, or to whom, or when—determine designation. Different facts are relevant for different indexicals, and the meaning of the indexical determines which. Names don't work like this. The difference between 'David' and 'Harold' is not that they are tied, by their meanings, to different relationships to the utterance or utterer. The role of context is simply to help us narrow down the possibilities for the permissive conventions that are being exploited.[31]

If we have to give this phenomenon a familiar name, it would be 'ambiguity'. The same name has many different meanings; as with ambiguous expressions, the role of context is to help us determine which meaning is relevant in a given use, rather than to supply a specific type of fact called for by the relevant meaning. There are many differences between the phenomenon in question and what we usually call 'ambiguity', however. Paradigm ambiguous expressions have only a few meanings, most of which are known to people who use the expression, or can be easily found by looking in a good dictionary. One can realistically aspire to knowing most of the meanings of many words. In contrast many names have thousands of meanings—that is, there are thousands of individuals that they are used to designate, exploiting various permissive conventions. People who use a given name will be ignorant of the vast majority of its meanings, and it would be

---

[31] In 'Words' (1990) David Kaplan develops an account of names that takes each naming convention to concern a different name. Rather than hundreds of thousands of meanings for 'David' we have hundreds of thousands of homophonic names. My approach seems more natural, at least to me. I don't see that Kaplan's move solves problems; it trades one epistemological problem for another: nambiguity (which meaning is used?) for identity (which name is used?). This shift could be absorbed by the reflexive-referential theory, however, for those who find the 'many-names' approach congenial.

silly to aspire to know most of them. For help in discovering or narrowing the possibilities in particular cases one might use a phone book, or even an encyclopedia, but not a dictionary. It is thus a bit misleading to say that names are ambiguous. I offer a pair of ugly terms, *nambiguous* and *nambiguity*, to remind us of both the similarities and differences between the case with names and paradigm cases of ambiguity.

So with names we have nambiguity, something like ambiguity, rather than indexicality. Nevertheless, we can define a useful concept of reflexive truth conditions for statements involving names.

6.4 Names and cognitive significance

Consider a case in which I see

(38)   David uses LISP

spray painted on a wall that I pass on my way to work in the morning. I infer an utterance, an act of graffiti production, call it **g**. I have no idea which David is being designated. So I have no idea what proposition is expressed by the graffiti, no idea of what its official content might be. But I can say under what conditions **g** is true.

(P^{x}38):   The person the convention exploited by **g** permits one to designate with 'David' uses LISP.

(P^{x}38) is not the proposition expressed by **g**—not **g**'s official content. But it does give truth conditions for **g**. And (P^{x}38) is reflexive; that is, it is a proposition about the very utterance of which it is the truth conditions.

Now let us suppose that **g** is actually a remark about David Israel, spray painted on the wall by a gang of teen-age admirers. In that case the content of **g** is a singular proposition about David Israel, and quite a different proposition than (P^{x}38). But (P^{x}38) is a proposition we want to have available, as part of our explanation of the impact of the perception of this message has on me.

Suppose I am irritated with the graffiti, and want to find out who did it. I start with (P^{x}38) and common sense. The author or authors of **g** were exploiting a convention that connected a particular David with their use of 'David'. Probably, they were either trying to insult this person or express admiration for him by associating him with LISP, a computer language based on the lambda calculus that appeals to philosophically inclined computer scientists. This David uses LISP (or at least might be accused of such a thing). And the graffiti writers in my neighborhood are in a position to exploit a convention that permits them to refer to him with 'David'. This might allow me to figure out who the graffiti was about—I ask around the neighborhood to see if anyone knows a computer scientist named David who either uses LISP or would be shocked to be accused of such a thing. Once I track down David, I ask him who might be spray painting things on walls about his programming habits.

Now let's return to Case 2. This is the case in which David utters (5) because he doesn't want his interlocutor to know that he is talking to David Israel, although he doesn't mind if he learns that the David Israel he is asking about is a computer scientist. We imagined that the interlocutor had a list of SRI employees, and he was going down the list.

What does the bureaucrat learn when he sees the name 'David Israel' on the list of people who work at SRI? In effect:

(39)   David Isreal works at SRI.

The official content of the statement made by the presence of Israel's name on the list is the singular proposition that Israel works at SRI. It would be misleading to say that this is what the interlocutor learns, however, since we are supposing he is merely a bureaucrat who has never heard of David Israel and has no concept of him except that he gains in virtue of seeing his name on the list. He has no way of thinking of Israel except as 'the person designated by this use of 'David Israel', which in terms of our account comes to 'the person whom the conventions exploited by this use of 'David Israel' allow us to call 'David

Israel'. We might then say that the bureaucrat does not fully grasp the meaning of the statement he is inspecting (which I'll call **h**). He knows the conventions associated with 'works at SRI' and he knows the type of convention associated with the use of 'David Israel', so he knows quite a bit. But he doesn't know everything. What he knows is,

(P^{x}39):   That the person the convention exploited by **h** permits one to designate with 'David Israel' works at SRI.

Now the bureaucrat formulates his question: 'What does David Israel do?' In asking this question, the bureaucrat exploits the convention that governs the token of 'David Israel' on the list of SRI employees he is using. It is interesting that he can do this. He doesn't know the convention *as* a convention for calling a certain person by a name, but only *as* the convention that is governing a certain use of the name. As far as he knows, he has never been face-to-face with the person designated by that token. It may be surprising, if one has certain philosophical predispositions, that the bureaucrat can ask a question the official content of which has David Israel as a constituent, a question which is *about* David Israel, when he knows so little about him. But this seems scarcely deniable. The bureaucrat seeks to be a conduit, taking information about Israel from person in front of him, who he assumes to have some richer level of acquaintance and interaction with Israel than he himself has, and passing it on down the line until it will be used by someone who also has a richer level of acquaintance or can gain it, say by summoning Israel to an office for an interview.

To achieve this purpose, the bureaucrat needn't know who Israel is, by any normal standards at least. What he does need to do is to make sure that the David Israel he has been asked to gather information about is the same one that the person in front of him is going to tell him about. He needs to make sure that the conventions governing his use of 'David Israel' are the ones governing its use in the reply he gets. He might do that by asking, "Do you know a person named 'David Israel' who works here at SRI? Do you know more than one?" If David answers appropriately he goes on to ask, "And what does David Israel do?"

David replies with (5). The reflexive truth conditions of (5) are that

(P^{x}5):   That *the person the convention exploited by* (5) *permits one to designate with 'David Israel'* is a computer scientist.

David's plan is that the bureaucrat, being a competent English speaker, will grasp (P^{x}5). He will assume that David is being helpful, and exploiting the same naming convention that he is— the same one the question on the form he is filling out exploits. This enables him to answer the question on his form. So David is helpful. But nothing in the transaction provides the interlocutor with information that David Israel is the person that is speaking to him. So, the level of reflexive content enables us to complete our story, and see how by using (5) David can expect to satisfy the combination of beliefs and desires that he had in Case 2.

6.5 Reflexivity and names

We have appealed to reflexive content to solve both parts of our problem, (P^{x}4) for (4) and (P^{x}5) for (5):

(P^{x}4)   That *the speaker of* ι is a computer scientist.

(P^{x}5)   That *the person the convention exploited by* (5) *permits one to designate with 'David Israel'* is a computer scientist.

Although (P^{x}4) and (P^{x}5) are both reflexive there is an important difference between them. (P^{x}4) is indexical content of (4), and so by the arguments so far, we can use it in explaining the cognitive significance of (4). But unless we treat names as indexicals, we can't argue that (P^{x}5) is the indexical content of (5).

It is somewhat tempting to treat names as indexicals. As I mentioned, I know of two David Kaplans, one the distinguished logician, the other a distinguished physician in Stanford's School of Medicine. So the name 'David Kaplan' designates different men in different conversations in which I am involved. Could we not treat it as an indexical? And would this not help us in dealing with puzzle cases involving names rather than indexicals? Or, to take a more traditional example, we could distinguish between the contents$_M$ of 'Cicero is a famous orator' and 'Tully was a famous orator', and solve this puzzle along the same lines used in the indexical cases.

But the problem with the two David Kaplans is not that there is a single word with a single meaning, that directs us to determine designation in terms of different contextual facts. It is rather nambiguity: there are a multiplicity of relatively local naming conventions that are relevant in different conversations; the role of context is pre-semantic, to help us figure out which convention is being exploited. The locality of these conventions made the case rather different from straightforward ambiguity, but the principle is the same. To grasp the meaning relevant to a particular use of 'David Kaplan'—to grasp the relevant convention—is just to grasp who is designated.   And so, to consider the famous example, the indexical contents of 'Cicero is a famous orator' and 'Tully is a famous orator' are the same. The level of indexical content is of no more use in explaining the different cognitive significance than the levels of designational or referential content. Once the meaning is fixed, the designation is fixed, the same for 'Tully' and for 'Cicero'. We get no explanation of the difference between the two statements with any of our three kinds of content.

And so, indexical content or content$_M$ does not provide what we need to understand (5). On the account of proper names we have developed, they are not treated as indexicals. The content$_M$ of (5) is the same as the content$_C$ of (5): (P^{r}5), the proposition that David Israel is a computer scientist.

It seems that (P^{x}5) provides what we need, but where do we fit it into our theory? (P^{x}5) doesn't give us any of the three kinds of content we have identified.

What ($P^x 5$) gives us is the truth conditions of (5) given *some* but not *all* of the facts about the meaning of (5). (5) tells us what else has to be true, given the facts about the meaning of 'is a computer scientist' and the fact that 'David Israel' is a proper name, but not given the facts about the specific conventions being exploited by the subutterance of this name. We might call this the "content$_M$ of (4) except for 'David Israel'."

This concept of truth conditions, truth conditions with part of the meaning fixed, is very important in the epistemology of language. It gets at what we know in a familiar and inevitable situation—when we know the meaning of some but not all of the words in an utterance. We use this level of content in planning our utterances, when we explain the meaning of a word by using it in a sentence. We rely on our interlocutor knowing the meaning of the sentence except for the word. So their grasp of the truth conditions of what we say will be the content$_M$ of our utterance *except for* this word. If we choose our example well, our interlocutor will be able to figure out the content of the statement as a whole. From this she can figure out what contribution the word must be making, and learn its meaning.

This mechanism is at work in the simple case in which we introduce ourselves. I meet you at a party, extend my hand, and say "I am John." You learn yet another permissive convention for 'John', that it can be used to designate me. You start out not knowing this convention. Assuming sincerity, and relying on what you already know, you learn the reflexive proposition, that there is a convention that allows one to call the speaker of the utterance you are hearing 'John'. You see that I am the speaker, and learn that I am named John. If referentialism is correct, the proposition I express is the metaphysically trivial. But who cares? That proposition is not the one my plan relies on.

When our student traveled to Princeton to meet David Lewis, she already knew the convention that allowed one to call David Lewis 'David Lewis'. She had a notion of a certain person, whose papers she had studied and whom she knew to be a professor at Princeton. When David introduced himself at the train station, she learned that the speaker, the person in front of her that was talking to her, was the well-known philosopher, David Lewis. To get at the cognitive impact of Lewis's statement on her—how it differed from his saying "I am I" or "David Lewis is David Lewis" —we need more than the indexical content, content$_M$. To understand how she combines what she already knows with what she learns from the utterance, we need to take as her starting point the reflexive contents with the meaning of 'David Lewis' only partly fixed. She learns that the speaker of the utterance she hears is named 'David Lewis'. Perception tells her that the speaker is the person she sees, and common sense and her knowledge of philosophy tells her that the only person named David Lewis in the Princeton department, or at least the only one likely to introduce himself as David Lewis without explaining that he was not *the* David Lewis, is David Lewis. So she infers that the convention that the person in front of her is exploiting is the one she already knows, and, he is David Lewis—the David Lewis whose articles she has read.

For a final example, let's return to the case of the two David Kaplans. Imagine the following. I am at a party, talking with a group of colleagues about the physician named David Kaplan that I mentioned above. I think Dr. Kaplan should be Stanford's next president, we may suppose, and I am extolling his virtues for this position. I see my wife Frenchie approaching. I know that when she hears the name 'David Kaplan' she will assume that we are talking about the logician, and will probably say something like,

> David Kaplan so loves his garden in Pacific Palisades, and he knows how to keep a healthy perspective on his work at the university.

I know that these remarks will totally undermine the case I am making for Dr. Kaplan. Who wants a president of Stanford who enjoys gardening in Los Angeles, much less one who knows how to keep his university work in perspective? I turn to Frenchie, and say,

> David Kaplan is a doctor in Stanford's School of Medicine.

Now what I have thereby said (content$_C$) is that a certain individual is a doctor in the medical school. I have not said that his name is 'David Kaplan', nor that he is the current topic of conversation, nor that the logician is not. What I said—the official content—is a proposition true in worlds in which the doctor has a different name, I have never discussed him, and the logician Kaplan was never born. Nevertheless, what I plan to convey to Frenchie is,

> In this conversation, John is not using 'David Kaplan' to designate David Kaplan our old friend.

How does my plan work? I plan on her reasoning something like this:

(i)   Assume John's utterance is true.

(ii)   John's utterance is true iff there is a unique person John is using 'David Kaplan' to designate and he is a doctor in Stanford's School of Medicine.

(iii)   So, there is a unique person John is using 'David Kaplan' to designate and he is a doctor in Stanford's School of Medicine.

(iv)   Our old friend David Kaplan is not a doctor in anyone's School of Medicine.

(v)   So, in the subutterance, John is not using 'David Kaplan' to designate our old friend David Kaplan.

(vi)   John is using 'David Kaplan' in this utterance as he is using it in the ongoing conversation.

(vii)   So in the ongoing conversation, John is not using 'David Kaplan' to designate our old friend David Kaplan.

The key to this plan is that on the basis of her trust in me (i) and her knowledge of English (ii) Frenchie will grasp (iii). (iii) plus common sense will lead her to (vii).

(iii) is certainly not what I said with my remarks: it is not content$_C$. But (iii) is also not content$_M$. It is the content *given* the facts that fix the meanings of everything except 'David Kaplan'.

(ii) reflects a true principle about English, which a linguistically competent person who knows (the rest) of English and recognizes that 'David Kaplan' is a proper name will accept. This is the situation Frenchie was in. She didn't know which meaning of 'David Kaplan' I was using, which permissive convention for the use of 'David Kaplan' I was exploiting. But she did know the general principles of how names contribute to the truth-conditions of the statements of which they are a part.

So at step (iii), I planned on Frenchie grasping the truth-conditions of my utterance *given* the facts that fix the meanings of everything but the name 'David Kaplan'.

(iii) is reflexive content, and content Frenchie grasps because of her linguistic competence. It is fair game to use it in an account of the epistemology of language. The epistemology of language without reflexive content, and the interplay of knowledge about the utterance and knowledge about the world that it reflects, is hopeless. Indexicality is not the same as reflexivity, but a large part of its importance to the philosophy of language is to help us to appreciate reflexivity.

6.6 Paderewski

A famous example of Kripke's (1979) involves the Pole Paderewski, famous both as a pianist and as a statesman. It is conceivable that someone, Elwood, say, should know of Paderewski as a statesman, and Paderewski as a pianist, without knowing that the pianist and the statesman are the same. There is no mystery about what goes on in Elwood's mind. He has two notions, one associated with the idea of being a pianist, among other things, and the other associated with the idea of being a statesman, among other things. Both are associated with the property of having the name 'Paderewski'. Elwood thinks he has to be careful when he hears the name 'Paderewski'. He thinks he has to to determine whether it is the pianist or the statesman that is being talked about. There is also nothing mysterious about the effect one might want to achieve, by telling Elwood, 'Paderewski is Paderewski'. One wants to link Elwood's two notions, so that he will merge them and there will be just one notion in Elwood's head, associated with all of the ideas associated with the two notions, or at least as many of them as can be consistently and plausibly combined.

The question is how one achieves that effect. A simple way would be to say, "there is only one Pole (at least only one that you have ever heard of) named 'Paderewski'." Or, using the name as a common noun, 'there is only one Paderewski', meaning much the same thing. But how does one convey this information, as one surely can, by saying (40)?

(40)   Paderewski is Paderewski

In some situations, this might be very similar to the case of Stretch. There might be two quite salient starting points for cognitive paths that both lead to Paderewski, and the first utterance of the name might be linked to one, the second to another. For example, one might first point to a poster announcing a concert by Paderewski, and then to a newspaper headline about a political event involving Paderewski.

But suppose, standing before the poster and the newspaper kiosk, one simply says, without demonstrating, 'Paderewski is Paderewski'. The reflexive content is

(P^x40)   That *the person associated with 'Paderewski' by the conventions exploited by the first use of that name in* **(40)** is *the person associated with 'Paderewski' by the conventions exploited in the second use of the name in* **(40)**.

Elwood figures out that the convention exploited by the poster is the same one exploited by the headline. This relies on the premise that the speaker is exploiting the same convention as the poster in one use of 'Paderewski' and the same convention as the headline in the other. This relies on Gricean considerations, that the speaker is attempting to say something relevant and helpful. Since the relation of identity is symmetrical, Elwood doesn't have to decide which use of 'Paderewski' is associated with the piano concert and which with the headline.

And in fact, given a certain amount of uptake on Elwood's part, the same effect can be achieved by saying "Paderewski is Paderewski" when there are no salient concert posters or newspaper headlines. This would work best if there were some discourse by Elwood that was salient, whose structure was explained by his not knowing that the pianist and the statesman were one. Suppose Elwood has just said, "I wonder if Paderewski the pianist and Paderewski the statesman are related."

Elwood's interlocutor could tell that Elwood meant to be exploiting two naming conventions, one for each use of 'Paderewski'. Other things being equal, Elwood can expect that the interlocutor will use the same conventions in responding to him as he used in asking his question, in which case the truth of 'Paderewski is Paderewski' will mean that there is only one person who is both statesman and pianist. Note that without this assumption, that in his reply the speaker has exploited all of the conventions Elwood exploited in his question, the truth of 'Paderewski is Paderewski' wouldn't exclude two Paderewskis. Ordinarily it wouldn't be very helpful to reply "Paderewski is Paderewski," if there were two Paderewskis, but it might nevertheless be true if one is exploiting only one or the other of the conventions. Perhaps the speaker also doesn't know that there is only one Paderewski, but nevertheless is passionate about the situation. He thinks that the statesman should never have been allowed to share a name with the great pianist, and simply refuses to use the name to refer to the statesman. He says,

Paderewski is Paderewski

while thinking to himself, "the statesman on the other hand, shouldn't have been allowed to share a name with the pianist, and I won't use the poor excuse of a convention that permits this."

This remark might be rather unhelpful but not false. In fact, Elwood is likely to misunderstand his interlocutor, and think he has been told that there is only one Paderewski, thus coming to believe the truth in spite of his interlocutor's ignorance.

6.7   Mach and the shabby pedagogue

Let's return to the case of Ernst Mach seeing himself in the mirror on the streetcar without realizing it. Our account of the cognitive significance of indexicals and names allows us to explain the difference among the assertions (1), (2), and (3).

(1)   That man is a shabby pedagogue

(2)   I am a shabby pedagogue

(3)   Mach is a shabby pedagogue

These statements all have the same referential content, the proposition consisting of Mach and the property of being a shabby pedagogue. But at the levels relevant to cognitive significance they differ.

While the utterances (1), (2) and (3) all require Mach to be a shabby pedagogue, the reason for this differs. The meaning of (1) determines that it will be true if its speaker is attending to a shabby pedagogue; it is the fact that the speaker is attending to himself that makes the speaker and the subject be the same. The meaning of (3), with the meaning of 'Mach' partly fixed, requires that the speaker be exploiting a convention that allows one to refer to someone with 'Mach' who is in fact a shabby pedagogue. It is the fact that Mach is the speaker, and that the convention he is exploiting allows one to refer to him with 'Mach', that requires the speaker and the subject be the same. But with (2) it is the meaning alone that determines that (2) is true if the speaker is a shabby pedagogue. The identity between the speaker and the

referent of the subject of the statement is a matter of the meaning
of the sentence in (2), and so is fixed at the level of content$_M$.

In this sense, then, (2) can be seen as a way of making a
self-assertion in a sense that (1) and (3) are not. The meaning
of (2) suits it to be a way for each person, whatever her name,
and whatever she is attending to, to say of herself that she is
a shabby pedagogue. And for this reason, his utterance of (2)
places a different cognitive load on Mach, than do his utterances
of (1) and (3). To utter (1) sincerely, Mach needs to believe that
the person he is attending to is a shabby pedagogue. To utter (3)
sincerely, he needs to believe that the person named by his use
of 'Mach' is a shabby pedagogue. He does not need to believe
either of these things to sincerely assert (2). But he does need to
believe that the speaker of the utterance he is making is a shabby
pedagogue.

This account takes a loan on the concept of self-belief; we
understand what is special about the cognitive load of (2) only
insofar as we understand what it is to have a belief about oneself;
that is, a belief about one not as the person one sees, or refers
to with a name that happens to be one's own, but a belief about
oneself *as* oneself. But what does this mean?

The question remains whether there is something peculiarly
mysterious about self-knowledge of the sort expressed by (2),
that we haven't provided the tools for analyzing. I argue that by
applying the concept of reflexivity to the apparatus of notions and
ideas, we can remove the mystery from self-knowledge (which is
not to say we can remove all the mysteries connected with the
self).[32]

6.8   What *is* said?

Considered at the referential level, identity statements which are
true are necessarily true, and those which are false are necessarily
false. The necessity of identity is now a commonplace, mainly
due to Kripke's work, especially *Naming and Necessity*. It was not

---

[32]See Perry, 1990a; Perry, 1998a; Perry, forthcoming.

always so. When Marcus's systems of modal logic included the necessity of identity, she found few supporters (1946; 1961). And before *Naming and Necessity* a standard position on the mind-body problem was that brain states were *contingently* identical with mental states, this contingent identity being reflected in the empirical inquiry necessary to discover such identities.

But if A is identical with B, then there is only one thing, a thing that is A and is B. Since Venus is identical with the morning star there is only one thing that is both Venus and the morning star. Since Cicero was identical with Tully, there was only one person that was Tully and was Cicero. The law of non-contradiction says that if a thing has a property it doesn't fail to have it too. So if A is necessarily identical with A, then so is B. One can't find a world in which A is not B, for there is only one thing to find; it is either in a world or it isn't. This much is pretty clear. We need then to allow for the metaphysical necessity of identity while allowing for the empirical nature of the knowledge we express. As Kripke points out, explicitly, forcefully and effectively, the statements that express necessary propositions aren't always knowable *a priori*.

So far I have been maintaining that our ordinary conception of *what is said* is official content, content with meaning and reference fixed. Combined with the view that true identity statements involving names and indexicals express necessary propositions, we get the result that what is said by making such statements is necessary. But we have seen that what one intends to convey with such statements is usually empirical and contingent. In our conversation about Stretch, I was conveying something to you that you couldn't figure out *a priori*, and that wasn't necessary: that there was but one dog behind the pillar. When David Lewis introduces himself by saying, "I am David Lewis" he doesn't intend to convey the necessary truth that David Lewis is David Lewis, but rather that his name is 'David Lewis', and, by conveying that, that he is a person already known to the student in other ways. It seems odd that it should turn out that what is said almost always

NAMES AND THE CO-REFERENCE PROBLEM / 119

with a form of words is almost never what one intends to convey.

Here is one way we can look at it. It's true that statements provide a system of contents, that vary in what he hold fixed. But these contents are not equal. Language has a core function, which is not to convey information about utterances, or about words, or about languages, or about meanings, or about context, but about the things the words stand for, their subject matter. The reflexive contents are possible because of the architecture of language. The way I communicate information about, say, Clinton's food preferences is by uttering words, in a language, with meanings, in a context to express a proposition:

(41)   Clinton likes hamburgers.

Given how language is designed to provide information about subject matter, it simply turns out that the right context I might use this sentence to teach you what 'hamburger' means, or who 'Clinton' stands for, or what 'like' means. The properties I would be exploiting are the very ones that make the system work. Because 'Clinton' stands for Clinton, I can use it to refer to Clinton. By the same token, if you know to whom I am referring (the very salient man on TV so passionately eating hamburgers) I can use it to teach you whom the name refers to. The fact that language works in virtue of knowledge of these facts, and thus can be used, in certain circumstances, to convey these facts, does not belie the truth expressed metaphorically by saying that language was designed to allow us to communicate about the things it is about, not itself.

In the most central cases, then, referential content will get at the information the speaker wishes to convey. What is said is what is said about the subject-matter; it is how the world has to be for the statement to be true, *given* the facts about meaning and reference. But the very nature of language gives rise to sentences the meaning of which guarantees they will not fit the general picture. Identity statements using names and indexicals are a case in point. They will virtually never be used with the intent of conveying their referential content, which will always be necessarily true or necessarily false.

Compare (41) with (42) and (43):

(42)   Bill Clinton is taller than Hillary Clinton

(4)   Bill Clinton is Bill Blythe

I utter (41) and (42) in a standard situation, as a way of telling someone who knows who 'Clinton' stands for about his food preferences, and a way of telling someone who knows who 'Bill Clinton' and 'Hillary Clinton' stand for about their comparative heights. (43) is uttered in the circumstances imagined in chapter 1: telling a childhood friend of Clinton's, who knew him by the name 'Bill Blythe' but is unaware of what happened to him in later life, that he is the same person as the president. In both cases, the speaker's plan does not end with expressing a proposition. With (41) the speaker wants to influence the listener's notion of Bill Clinton, associating it with the idea of liking hamburgers. With (42) the speaker intends to influence two of the listen's notions, his Bill notion and his Hillary notion. And this is also the case with (43). The speaker wants to influence two of the listener's notions, his Clinton notion and his Blythe notion.

Suppose now in all three cases my listeners believe me, and hence their beliefs change, and they come to believe something they didn't believe. In the first two cases this means that the *referential* truth-conditions of their set of beliefs will have changed. In order for their beliefs to be true, Clinton will have to like hamburgers, and have to be taller than Hillary.

In contrast, the change in beliefs I induce with (43) will not change the *referential* truth-conditions of the listener's beliefs (at least not until he starts to make some inferences). Given the referential facts about his notions, there was no way for his beliefs to be true without it being true that his Clinton and Blythe notions were of the same person. This was guaranteed by the fact that they were notions of the same person; there was therefore only one person to serve as the referent of both; there was not way they could fail to co-refer, once the facts of reference are fixed; there was no way consistent with his beliefs, given the facts of reference, that his thought 'Clinton *isn't* Blythe' could be true. His new belief, 'Clinton is Blythe,' induced by my saying (43), does change things, however. The change is at the reflexive level. If we abstract from the reference of his notions, there was nothing in his mind, before my remark, that required the two notions to co-refer. After the remark there was — some internal analogue to the identity sign[33]

In the case of such identities (and statements expressing other necessarily reflexive relations), referential contents do a very poor job of getting at the state of belief that the speaker expresses and intends to bring about. It is very odd to say that when I say "Bill Blythe is Bill Clinton," that I am expressing a necessary truth, or saying the same thing as I would say if I said "Bill Clinton is Bill Clinton." But surely one reasonable position is that this is simply an oddity that falls out the general use of a device, our concept of what is said, that usually does quite a satisfactory job of getting at what people use their words to convey.

We might say that given hypothesis that the standard function of language is to convey information about subject matter given referential facts, the hypothesis that this is the function which explains the most about why language evolved and how it is used, the test of a semantical theory will be getting the subject matter truth conditions straight. And given that perspective, the proposition that captures these truth-conditions has every claim on being the proposition that is expressed—at being, that is, 'what is said'.

Another position is worth considering, however. This is that the concept of what is said is a bit less straightforward than this. Perhaps the referential content is the *default* candidate for what is said, but in certain circumstances other levels of content can be, as I will put it, *raised to subject matter*. In cases where referential content will always be trivially and necessarily true or false, the

---

[33]I call this 'internal identity' in Perry, 1980.

default is overridden. Identity statements trigger the mechanism that replaces the default. We raise some salient empirical content to subject matter. We'll return to this suggestion in chapter 8, when considering the content of existence statements.

Names, Networks and Notions

7.1 Introduction

The name 'Jacob Horn' comes from the book, *The Horn Papers*, which was published as if it were the newly discovered diary of a colonist, but was in fact made up. So Jacob Horn does not exist. That is, the statement

(44)   Jacob Horn does not exist

is true.

The example comes from Keith Donnellan. In 'Speaking of Nothing,' he provides the following rule for determining the truth-value of a statement of the form 'N exists' where N is a proper name.

> If N is a proper name that has been used in predicative statements with the intention to refer to some individual, then 'N does not exist' is true if and only if the history of those uses ends in a block. (25)[34]

Donnellan explains a block as follows:

> When the historical explanation of the use of a name (with the intention to refer) ends ... with events that preclude any referent being identified, I will call it a 'block' in the history. (23)

Think of the history of a use as a stream of events that leads up to that use. In determining the referent of a use of 'Jacob Horn' we go upstream, back in time, looking for an object that plays the

---

[34]I've used single quotes where Donnellan uses corner quotes.

right role to be the referent. Sometimes we don't make it back to such an object. There is an event that blocks us. In the case of 'Jacob Horn' the event is finding someone writing *The Horn Papers* not as a real diary but as a fake diary. That's where the stream begins. No one in it plays the right role in its origin to be the referent of 'Jacob Horn'.

Donnellan's rule is reflexive in my sense. The truth condition for a statement containing an empty name is a condition on the utterance of the name in the statement: that *its* history end in a block. Donnellan's account is an instance of providing a reflexive truth-condition for a statement when a subject matter condition is not available. And Donnellan rather carefully does not claim that he is telling us *what is said* by a statement like (44). Donnellan's strategy is thus congenial to and in fact foreshadows the reflexive-referential theory.

Following Donnellan, I'll divide the problem of empty names into two parts: empty names in discourse about reality, and empty names in fictional discourse. I'll focus on reality in this chapter, but have a bit to say about fiction in the next. Donnellan intended the Jacob Horn example as an case of an empty name in discourse about reality. The *Diaries* were not presented as fiction, but as fact. In the beginning, people were fooled and intended to be talking about a real person, Jacob Horn, who actually did things, not a fictional character. The criterion of correctness for statement about Jacob Horn was *truth*—correspondence with the facts. The criterion for correctness in discourse about fiction is what I will call *accuracy:* basically correspondence to the the content of some canonical representations, such as the statements in a novel under discussion.

In this chapter I apply the reflexive-referential theory to the no-reference problem, as exemplified in the Jacob Horn case. We'll see that the machinery we have so far is incomplete, and needs to be supplemented in a way suggested by Donnellan's theory of blocks. In the chapter 6 the conventions involved in naming were thought of as involving names and the individual named. But we need an intermediate entity, which I call a notion-network. Notion-networks support the conventions needed to use names; some of these networks have origins of the sorts that supplies a referent for the name. The others contains blocks; being blocked is a characteristic of a notion-network. While I take my account to be in the spirit of Donnellan's, it also incorporates ideas from Evans (Evans, 1973), Kripke (Kripke, 1980), Kaplan (Kaplan, 1969) and others who have developed causal or historical accounts of reference.

Consider these statements:

(44)   Jacob Horn does not exist.

(45)   Jacob Horn exists

(46)   Jacob Horn was an important person in Colonial America

Intuitively, all of these statements are contingent; (44) is contingently true; Jacob Horn does not exist, but he might have. (45) and (46) are contingently false. This result falls out of the descriptive approach. Where JH is the identifying condition associated with 'Jacob Horn', (44) expresses the proposition that no one fits JH; (45) that someone does fit JH, and (46) that the person who does was an important person in Colonial America.

The intuitions do not accord with the naive referential approach, however. Combined with a structural approach to propositions, it finds that (45) and (46) fail to express propositions at all. Combined with a possible worlds approach, they express the necessarily false proposition, the empty set of worlds; since there is no Jacob Horn, there are no worlds in which Jacob Horn exists much less was an important person in Colonial America. Neither result seems satisfactory; the people who were fooled by the book seem to have believed something, and the something they believed seems like it might have been true.

Even if one can swallow the naive referential approach to (45) and (46), there seem to be serious problems with (44). (44)

is clearly true. What truth does the referentialist have for it to express? The natural way to interpret existence statements, an approach recommended by both Frege and Russell, is as asserting that certain condition have the higher order property of being instantiated. 'Ducks exist' means that the property of being a duck is instantiated. So we need a condition or property to interpret (44). Up to a point, the referentialist can adopt this approach to existence statements. If he has an object, he can get the condition of being identical with that object. What makes it true that Clinton exists is that there is someone who is identical with Clinton; the property or condition of being identical with Clinton is instantiated. But the approach does not help with empty names: if there is no individual, as in the Jacob Horn case, there is no condition of being identical with that individual, either.

7.2 Applying the reflexive-referential theory

As in the case of the co-reference problem, my initial recommendation is that the referentialist retreat to reflexive content to find the conditions missing at the referential level of content. The level we want is the content given all the facts about meaning and context given, except the individual meaning of 'Jacob Horn'. Thus we obtain:

(P^{x}44a) That there is no person that is assigned to *the convention being exploited by the use of 'Jacob Horn' in* (44).

(P^{x}45a) That there is a person that is assigned to *the convention being exploited by the use of 'Jacob Horn' in* (45).

(P^{x}46a) That there is a person that is assigned to *the convention being exploited by the use of 'Jacob Horn' in* (46), and he was an important Colonial American.

These propositions have the features that were intuitively associated with (44), (45) and (46). (P^{x}44a) is true, but contingently so. There are worlds in which the convention involved in the discourse using the name 'Jacob Horn' are not 'blocked'; in which we find a real person being named and not merely an inventive author at the beginning of the process that leads to the use of 'Jacob Horn'. And (P^x45a) and (P^x46a) are contingently false; false because there in fact in no one that meets the condition, contingent because there might have been.

As in the case of the reflexive treatment of the problem of co-reference, this will be unsatisfying to some, because the subject matter of (44), (45), and (46) should not include the conventions and utterances. These are not the possibilities we were thinking of. My answer here is essentially the same. The possibilities that are thinkable have to do not only with the distribution of properties over the things we think about (the subject matter of our thoughts) but also with the way those thoughts fit into the world. To squeeze the second sorts of thoughts into the first mode is to commit what I call the subject matter fallacy.[35]

There is, however, another problem. The concept of a convention I introduced in the last chapter will not bear the weight being put on it here. If a convention permits a name to be used to refer to an individual, how can we have a convention, where there is no individual? There are many David Kaplans in the world; on my view, we have one name, and many conventions. What makes the conventions different, on the conception of a convention used in the last chapter, is simply the different individuals involved. The different conventions are assignments of different individuals to the same name. But that conception won't work here. In the Jacob Horn case there is no individual involved. To see the point, imagine that the same name, 'Jacob Horn', had been used by two different hoaxers; in addition to the Jacob Horn that was supposed to be a Colonial American, another Jacob Horn was introduced in another book, purporting to be a Civil War veteran. The same name would be part of two different conventions; but what makes the conventions different? It can't be the individuals named, for the name is empty in both cases.

---

[35]See Perry, 2001a.

The natural place to turn to explain the difference in the two uses is the different processes, the different communicative chains, that led to them, one starting with one hoaxer, the other with the other. The original impulse for recognizing such communicative chains in referential theories of proper names was to simply to provide an alternative to the descriptive account of how a name could be connected with a particular person or thing. Donnellan's theory suggests, however, that the process that intervenes between the individual names and the use of the name might itself have interesting and useful properties, and be a worthy object of theorizing. Similar ideas come from Evans's work on names (1973) and from Kripke's work (1980).[36]

In the balance of this chapter, I construct an account of such chains. Then in the next chapter, we return to the question of applying the reflexive-referential theory to empty names.

7.3 Intersubjective networks of notions

In this section, I develop the concept of an *intersubjective network of notions* (*notion-network* for short). The basic picture is simple. We learn about objects through perceptions. When we perceive things, we have ideas of them (notions), that we associate with ideas for the properties we perceive them to have, creating a sort of internal file (a notion associated with ideas). Thus the first link in our networks: perceptions of objects give rise to notions, and information flows from perception to notion. We retain these files when we are no longer perceiving the objects — the detach and recognize information game. We use language to share information that we gain in this way. Hence, the networks are intersubjective, involving notions and files that different people have of the same object. When we share information, the person doing the sharing constructs a statement with a reference in it, which is guided by the internal file he has of the object. This is the second kind of connection between nodes of the network: from notion to utterance. The person receiving the information has a

---

[36]See also Perry, 1980.

perception of the utterance. On the basis of it, he starts a new file or adds to one he already has. This is the third sort of connection, from perception of an utterance to notion.

I see these networks as having much in common with the structures along which information flows.[37] What flows along them is not restricted to information, however. Information is supposed to be true, and to be guaranteed to be true, and that simply isn't always the case with the ideas we pass along through language. I'll use the word 'content' instead of information.

Let's look a bit more closely at these types of nodes.

Object-perceptions

I take perceptions to be sensations structured by ideas and notions. Right now I am perceiving my computer. I have a complex visual sensation, which I interpret with my ideas, such as the ideas of being a computer, being a table, of being one thing resting on another, of being a keyboard, etc. So I perceive a computer resting on a table with a keyboard in front of it. I could conceivably have this sensation, or something very like it, without knowing that I was seeing a computer, or that the thing I saw was separable from the table beneath, and so forth.

Notions, buffers and files

I assume that the Greeks, on the basis of perceptions *of* the Parthenon, formed *notions* of it. They associated various ideas with their notions, such as being a big building at the Acropolis, being a temple to Athena, being the place where one applies for licenses to practice rhetoric, and so forth. So Thrasymachus may be rushing to the Parthenon, believing that is the place he can get a license to teach argumentation, and hoping that it is still open.

References and statements

References are parts of utterances. Utterances are intentional acts, which I regard as *cognitive* particulars even though they often involve observable bodily movements. In this chapter I'll mainly be thinking about the utterance of a simple indicative sentence

---

[37]See the works listed in footnote 4.

containing a singular term with the intention of communicating content; I'll call such utterances *statements*.

References and statements are guided by notions and the files that are associated with them. Paradigmatically, a speaker wants to communicate to a listener that an object has a certain property. The speaker wants the listener to have an appropriate notion of the object associated with an idea of the same type as the speaker has associated with his notion. For example, you ask me a question about computers. I say to you, pointing at David, "He is a computer scientist." I want you to associate the idea of being a computer scientist with a notion that is attached to your perception of David. I think this change in your cognitive state will motivate you to approach David with your question.

Reference-perceptions

These are perceptions that are suited to being perceptions of references. The buffers connected with these perceptions are keyed to references and anaphoric chains of references, providing a home for the information picked up until an identification is made or the buffer is converted to a detached notion. When you hear me say "David," you form a buffer of the person I am referring to. When you collect enough information to figure out to whom I refer, this buffer is absorbed into the permanent file for that person. Adept speakers plan their utterances so that the listener will be able to make this identification. When talking on the phone, for example, they don't use demonstratives to refer to objects around them that their interlocutor can't identify. When using common names like 'David', they make sure that which David they refer to is clear from context, or supply additional information.

Etiological Structure: origins and parents

The way the nodes of notion-structures give rise to each other establishes what I call the etiology or pedigree. Notions arise in seven ways:

E-1) *Object-perceptions give rise to notions*. I'll call the object a perception is of its *origin*. When Thrasymachus saw Socrates,

Socrates was the origin of his perception. This property is preserved by the *parent* relation; that is, when one node gives rise to another, the origin of the first is the origin of the second. If Trasymachus's perception of Socrates gave rise to a notion, Socrates was the origin of that notion. When we perceive an object we don't immediately recognize we create a notion for it, and associate ideas with our new notion on the basis of what we perceive. This sort of notion is what I call a buffer. The perception is the parent of the buffer. If the perception has a origin (if there is an object it is a perception of), then that object is the *origin* of the notion also. This is an intrasubjective relation. The notion arises in the very mind that has the perception.

One can have a experience of the sort that is suited to be the perception of an object, but is caused by something else. For example, I have heard things that I took to be people knocking at the door, when no one was there. I have thought I have seen people approaching in the fog, when there was no one there. I have thought I felt a fish tug on my line, when there was no fish. So, in general, we need to make a distinction between perceptions that are (more or less) suited to be, and are taken to be, perceptions of objects, and ones that actually are of objects.

One could feel a tug on his line, perhaps due to a weed or a rock, see a quick shadow in the water, and think he was feeling a fish of which he could see the vague outline. He might surmise that it was a large bass, full of fight, at least four or five years old, that had lived near the log where he was fishing for a couple of years—one that he had hooked before, only to see it get away, as he thinks happens this time. He might name this old fish 'Houdini', and tell his friends about it, and they might tell their friends; in the end his fishing spot might be ruined by all the people trying to catch Houdini. The path back from 'Houdini' to a fish, though, would be blocked. So here is one sort of block we can have in a notion-network. We get to a perceptual event that gives rise to a notion, but which wasn't itself a real perception of an object. A skeptic might suppose that events something like this are responsible for names like 'Nessie' (Scotland's Loch Ness Monster), 'Yeti' (Nepal's Abominable Snowman) and 'Sasquatch' (the Pacific Northwest's Bigfoot). This is the first kind of block.

E-2) *Notions give rise to references.* When a notion gives rise to and governs a reference, the notion is the parent of the reference, and if the notion has a origin, it is also the origin of the reference. So, for example, if Thrasymachus's wants to tell Alcibiades about Socrates, his Socrates notion will leads him to refer and govern what he says; Socrates will be the origin of that reference. This again is an intrasubjective relation; the notion is in the mind of the person who refers.

E-3) *References give rise to perceptions of them.* Sometimes we perceive acts of referring (or tokens that are produced in the course of utterances, or copies of such tokens, or translations of copies of such tokens, or other even more remote traces of acts of referring).

This is an intersubjective relation; one person refers, another person perceives the reference. The reference is the parent of the perception of the reference, and the origin of the reference is the origin of the perception of the reference.

Sometimes an utterance that is not strictly act of referring triggers the same buffer-formation response. You say, "I saw an interesting man today." You haven't actually referred to the man you saw, or even strictly implied that there is only one. Maybe you just mean that of the thousands of men you saw today as you walked through the streets of San Francisco one was sure to be interesting. But probably you have someone in mind, and you are going to tell me more. I am likely to anticipate getting further information, and open a buffer for the person you have in mind. Even though you haven't referred, if I am right that you do have a man in mind, I can anaphorically co-designate that person: 'Tell me what made him interesting'. Of course, I might be wrong, and my buffer will turn out to be at best a rather short-lived notion network, with no parent and no offspring.

Just as one can seem to perceive an object that isn't there, one can seem to hear or see a statement or reference that doesn't occur. Emily Lattela was a character created by the gifted comedienne Gilda Radner during the heyday of the *Saturday Night Live* television show. Emily's special gift was misunderstanding things. Imagine Emily Lattella hearing 'Solipsism is a position, that philosophers try to avoid', as 'Sol Ipsism is a physician that philosophers try to avoid.' She tells all of her friends about this odd situation, and people begin sharing ideas and discoveries about what this doctor Sol Ipsism must be like, and why philosophers want to avoid him. Scholarship occurs, books are written, and so forth. So this is the second kind of a block.

E-4) *Reference-perceptions give rise to notions*. When we witness a statement—usually either hearing it or reading it—and we can't immediately identify the person or thing we are hearing or reading about, we create a buffer for the object referred to, and associate the ideas with our new notion on the basis of what we hear or read. The reference perception is the parent of the notion, and the origin of the new notion will be the origin of the reference perception, if there is one. This relation is intrasubjective; the notion arises in the mind of the person who perceives the reference.

Now we have all we need for the development of networks that last for thousands of years. Suppose I tell the students in my philosophy class about Socrates. My references are to Socrates (he is their origin) because they were guided by my notion of him (E-2). My notion has Socrates as its origin, because it was formed from perceiving references to him, probably by Will Durant in his book *The Story of Philosophy*, the first philosophy book I read (E-3). Durant's references were to Socrates because they were guided by his notion of Socrates (E-2), and so forth and so on back to someone whose notion of Socrates was formed by perceiving him (E-1). Perhaps there are not that many intervening steps. Durant may have first heard of Socrates by reading Plato's writings, and Plato may have formed his notion of Socrates on the basis of perception.

E-5) *Notions can be freely created.* So far we've encountered two ways in which one can end up with a notion without an origin. The pedigree can trace back to misperception of an object or of a reference. But notions can simply be created without origins, without any misperception or mistake of any other sort occurring. This is what happened in the Jacob Horn case, and in other cases in which fictional characters are invented. This is our third kind of block.

Freely created notions, and their offspring, can be involved in beliefs. This can be the result of a mistake, such as not realizing that the story one is being told is fiction. But one can also create a notion as a result of beliefs about individuals who will exist in the future. We'll encounter some examples of this below, when we discuss commandeering.

The free creation of notions is sometimes a cooperative, social enterprise, perhaps better described as the creation of a network without an origin. Some general principles, scientific breakthroughs, or felt cultural needs lead to the creation of a network of rich files, pretty much in agreement, about an object that will fit some description or play some role. One might think of various ideas of gods, messiahs, and other supernatural creatures that play various roles, such as giving gifts to deserving children on Christmas Eve, as examples of this.

E-6) *Notions can be merged.* It often happens that we have two notions of the same individual. For example, I may have read about Quine and have a very rich file on him. I then encounter him at an *APA* reception, without knowing who I am talking to. I form a notion, a buffer, of the person I am talking to. After a while I recognize that it is Quine, and absorb the buffer into my old notion of Quine. The two notions had different pedigrees that led to the same origin, Quine. The Quine network of the notion I had entering the reception started with him, led through various other people's perceptions of him and writings about him, and reached me via perception of their writings about Quine. The one I acquired when I saw him at the party had a much shorter pedigree, involving only E-1).

We can distinguish between cases in which a rather transitory notion, of the sort one forms when perceiving an object—what I'm calling a buffer—, is absorbed by a more permanent notion that retains its identity, and those that are better thought of as true mergers, two old notions combining to yield a new one. Suppose I have read a few articles by Harold McDuff. Harold retires to Palo Alto, and moves in down the street. I meet him and see him out for walks. But I don't connect him with the philosopher McDuff. When I finally straighten things out, I may have two equally rich files about McDuff, neither of which really gets absorbed into the other.

There is a lot of notion-merging in the early stages of a network. Various people form notions of a newcomer on the basis of their own perceptions, and notions of combine these with notions of of the newcomer gotten from others. Smith moves to town. Mrs. Jones across the street and Mr. Roberts next door see him at different times. Then Mrs. Jones and Mr. Roberts have a conversation and compare notes. Here we have two networks, with a common origin. (See also I-4). There are two networks, because there is no common parent between Mrs. Jones' notion of Smith and Mr. Roberts. When the conversation begins, however, all this changes. Mrs. Jones say, "the new neighbor..." Mr. Roberts forms a buffer of the person to whom Mrs. Jones is referring, and immediately combines it with his notion of Smith based on perception. This notion now has both his perception of Smith and Mrs. Jones' perception of Smith as parents. So now we have a single network.[38]

We can distinguish three situations in which files are combined. There is recognition of identity; the origins of two notions are the same, and the notions are combined. Then there are mistakes about identity, misrecognitions; the origins of two notions

---

[38]Contrary to what this might suggest, we not want to accept the general principle that any networks that share a node become a single network. This would mean that any time there is a case of misrecognition, networks get combined. I don't offer a general account of network individuation here.

are not the same, but they are combined. Finally there is something I'll call *identification-with*. This occurs when a real object is taken to be the object a freely created notion is about.

I call the result of a misrecognition a *mess*. Messes are our fourth sort of block. The simplest sorts of case involve perceptual misrecognition. I see David Israel across the street, but I don't recognize him. I take him to be Paul Newman. That is, I form a buffer based on perception the origin of which is Israel. When I think I recognize who it is this buffer feeds information into the Paul Newman file from my observations of Israel.

Messes can begin with language. Suppose you are standing in front of the philosophy department talking with your friends about Aristotle Onassis. I join the conversation and quite naturally take you to be talking about the philosopher. The issue under discussion is how much Aristotle knew about Plato, and I say, "Aristotle knew Plato and his philosophy very well." We might have a disagreement about what I have said. On one view, towards which I incline, I have inadvertently referred to and said something false about Onassis, although my statement was guided by my file about the philosopher. One can think of the use of names in conversations as akin to anaphoric co-designation. The speaker's intention to exploit the convention already in play trumps his intention to refer to the person his guiding notion is of. The case is structurally similar to 'directing intentions' in the use of demonstratives. I intended to refer to the philosopher Aristotle *by* exploiting the 'Aristotle' convention that was already in play. The lower level intention succeeds, but not the higher level one; by exploiting the convention in play, I refer to Onassis not, as I intended and thought, the philosopher. Alternatively, we could suppose that I have said something true about the philosopher that is irrelevant to the conversation. While *what I said* may be unclear, there is no mystery about what has happened. I opened a buffer for the person you were talking about and downloaded information to it from my Aristotle-the-philosopher file, which then guided my remark to you.

Identification-with occurs when a freely created notion with a relatively large file begins to be used to store information about a real object. A detective may have a very rich file on the murderer, before he identifies the murderer with a particular suspect. The file on Neptune was assembled on grounds of theory and inference before the planet was actually observed. The real object is *taken to be* the object for which the file was created. The freely created notion in effect *adopts* a parent that has an origin, and hence acquires an origin itself.

In this case, we have the first of two kinds of *diversions* we shall encounter. The word is supposed to suggest two things. First, the use of the file is diverted from its original use to being the receptacle of information about the adopted origin. Second, when we imagine going back along the historical chain, we are diverted from the path that leads to a freely created notion and a block, along the path that leads to perception of a real object and a bearer for the name.

This whole process is much more common and mundane than one might think. David Israel points out that it is common for parents to establish the names for their children before the children exist. Let's suppose the Browns, shortly after marriage, decide to call their first child 'Charles'. They are confident that they will have children, and that the first will be a male. They talk about what Charles will be like, where he will go to school, and the like. Eventually they have a child, it is a male, and they call it Charles. The discourse about Charles continues seamlessly, starting before conception, continuing through pregnancy, birth, childhood and beyond.

When did the name 'Charles' become Charles's name? When did the parents' discourse using the name 'Charles' begin to involve references to Charles? Only after Charles began to exist. A notion was freely created (E-5) on the basis of a an identifying condition, *our first child*. More ideas were associated with that notion, including the intention to name it 'Charles' and the belief that it would have that name. When the child began to exist that child was *taken to be* the child the notion and file were created for. The notion of the child based on perception was absorbed into the freely created file. As intentions tied to the notion were applied to the child—he was baptized 'Charles,' for example—, and information about the child gleaned from experience with him was stored by associating ideas with the notion, the notion *came to be* of the child.

A notion can be taken to be, and come to be, the notion of a particular object, even if the object doesn't meet the description with which the notion was associated when created. Perhaps Charles is a twin, whose older brother died in birth, so he really wasn't the couple's first child. Perhaps after struggles to conceive they adopted a child, or found a surrogate mother or father. Perhaps the mother's Charles-notion survived intact through a series of childless marriages before Charles finally came along, her first child but not the first child of the original couple.

E-8) *File-splitting*. Files can be split, so that we have two notions, each associated with some of the material in the previous file. This is what we do, if we can, when we realize we have made or inherited a mess.

I once discovered that I had combined information about two different people, both named 'Ellen Van Slyke', into a single file. There was no particular problem pulling the file apart, and creating two notions where there had been one. The striking thing about Ellen had been that although she was a very good student (according to the teaching assistant), she thought she needed an incomplete because she was doing so poorly (that's what she told me at office hours). Once I realized there were two distinct and quite different students, it was pretty easy to pull the file apart, creating one file of a good student I had never met, and one of a poor student who had talked to me but had never gone to sections and never met her teaching assistant. (Of course, it is also possible to find out that one has a file full of information and misinformation about two different individuals, without having any idea how to pull them apart.)

In a file-splitting case, there are two notions with the confused (or allegedly confused) file as parent. Now consider the parents of the confused file. In my case, there was a perceptual buffer of one Ellen, and a reference buffer from a reference by my TA to the other Ellen. One Ellen was the origin of one, the other Ellen the origin of the other. Are both of these buffers ancestors of both of the new notions? If so, then it seems that both of my notions have both Ellen Van Slykes as origins after things have been pulled apart. That is not what we want. We need to recognize the possibility of *disowning* as well as adopting. Think of disowning a parent (the mess) and adopting a grandparent as one's parent (one of the buffers). In this case, both of my new notions disown the mess; one adopts the perceptual buffer and the other the reference buffer. The first is the notion of the flaky student I met, the second the notion of the good student I didn't meet but heard about.

This is the second kind of diversion. Again, the word is meant to suggest two things. One of the files is diverted from the use of storing information about and guiding references to one Ellen, and the other is diverted from storing information about and guiding references to the other. And as we trace the chain back, we are diverted from the path to the wrong Ellen.

In the case I described, the relation is *intrasubjective*. However, file-splitting can also be a cooperative, social process. It may simply amount to *co-option*: a mess is repeatedly used to store information about one of its orgins, which becomes in time the 'dominant source' (Evans) of the file. The facts about the other origin become irrelevant to the use of the network, and disappear from the files in time.

Fictionalizing is a sort of dual of identifying-with. This happens when we create a fictional character based on the file of a real object. We take what we are interested in from the original file, throw away the uninteresting bits, and add what we want. We don't take the new file to have the origin that its parent did, but to be blocked—the fifth and last kind of block we shall meet in this chapter.

Content Flow

The second group of relations involve the flow of content from one node to another—ultimately, from a file of which a notion is a part, to a file of which another notion is a part.

A contentful state involves an idea of a property (or relation) associated with a node (or structure of nodes). The picture is this: *A* picks up information about an object by perceiving it. This takes the form of an idea of an perceived property becoming associated with a notion of the object. Then this information, perhaps together with other content, flows, via language, to person *B*; she ends up with the same idea associated with one of her notions, a notion of the same object, if things go right. Perhaps *A* sees that the Parthenon has lots of columns, and says to person *B*, "The Parthenon has lots of columns." The result of this is that person *B* associates the idea of having lots of columns with her idea of the Parthenon.

When we say the 'same idea' ends up associated with *B*'s Parthenon notion, however, we cannot mean the same cognitive particular. The picture is incoherent unless we appeal to some concept of *types* of ideas. So here I assume some more structure about notions and ideas. I assume that our ideas of properties and relations can be typed, so that we can speak meaningfully of particular ideas in different heads that are of the same type.

I also assume that we can have ideas of the same property or relation that are of different types, liable to being aroused by different perceptions and words. I want the following to make sense, for example. You and I both have an idea of (short-tailed) *weasel* and an idea of *ermine*, and neither of us know that 'weasel' and 'ermine' stand for the same kind of animal. Our ideas of ermines are of the same type, but my idea of weasel and my idea of ermine are not. When I see a dead weasel draped around a wealthy person's neck, one that was killed in the winter while its fur was white, my ermine idea is aroused but not my weasel idea. There are also empty ideas, such as those associated with the words 'bandersnatch' or 'jabberwock'.

I hope at some future time to develop an account of concepts and networks of ideas. It will be in some ways quite similar and in others rather more complicated than what I am saying about notion-networks here. But for now I try not to assume anything more about the nature of this typing here than I have indicated.

I want to call attention to seven facts about content flow:

I-1) *Content flows from perceptions of which object perceptions are a part to the files associated with notions.* (Intrasubjective) In the example above, Plato saw Socrates at various times in various places doing various things. He had perceptions of Socrates which were parts of larger perceptions. Content flowed from these perceptions to Plato's file of Socrates. On the admittedly oversimplified picture I am sketching here, Plato's first perception of Socrates also gave rise to his notion of Socrates. In that case there was both etiology and content flow. Later on, when Plato recognized Socrates, content flowed into the already existing file.

If Plato saw Thrasymachus and mistook him for Socrates, content would flow from his Thrasymachus perception into his perceptual buffer and from there into his Socrates file.

I-2) *Content flows from files to statements.* (Intrasubjective) Plato wrote about Socrates, his words being guided by his Socrates file. In this case, we have both creation of references and flow of content to the statements of which they are a part.

I-3) *Content flows from the statements to the perceptions of statements.* (Intersubjective) Durant read Plato's words about Socrates (or more likely copies of translations of copies of them). We are supposing Durant never had heard of Socrates until he read Plato. When he first came on a reference to Socrates, he formed a buffer for the reference of the term 'Socrates' as Plato was using it (E-3) with which ideas were associated based on what Plato's words said (I-3). The same thing happened over when I read Durant's words, and when my students heard my words.

I-4) *Content flows from perceptions of statements to files.* (Intrasubjective) When Durant read the words of Plato and others about Socrates, content from these statements flowed to his Socrates file.

Mistakes can occur at this point too. I might read a statement containing the name 'Roosevelt' that is in fact about Theodore Roosevelt and add the content to my Franklin Roosevelt file.

I-5) *Files are combined when notions are merged.* This may require some adjustments; resolution of inconsistencies, and inferences to conclusions warranted by the combined information.

I-6) *Files are separated when notions are split.* Some of the content may be thrown away. For example, in the Ellen Van Slyke case, I had drawn the conclusion that Ellen was insecure given her good performance and low opinion of herself as a philosophy student. But the data in the files didn't support that conclusion once I realized there was not a single person involved. There was just one good student who probably knew it, and one realistic lazy one.

I-7) *The fact that notions belong to the same network does not guarantee that content will flow between them.* You and I may both have our notions of Socrates from reading Will Durant's *Story of Philosophy.* But our notions may not be linked—that is, related in such a way that content will flow between them in at least one direction. For one thing, the perceptual events necessary for this to happen may never occur. I may never read what you have written or hear what you say about Socrates, for example, and vice versa. But also, I might hear you talking about Socrates, about the very same person that I know about, but not realize that's whom you are talking about.

A person could even have two notions of Socrates in his or her mind that were unlinked. This possibility is easier to see if we switch philosophers. Suppose that in Roman history courses Cicero is commonly called 'Tully' while in philosophy courses he is commonly called 'Cicero'. We can easily imagine a mentally unaggressive student, who takes courses from both departments and ends up with two unlinked notions of the same Roman. These two notions would be part of the same network that goes back to the discourse of Ancient Romans. In those days, I guess, everyone knew Marcus Tullius Cicero by all three of his names.

7.4   Networks and information games

When we take ourselves to be dealing with real objects, we treat our files in ways that reflect basic metaphysical principles about objects. We strive to keep our files self-consistent, reflecting the fact that objects cannot both have and not have a given property (non-contradiction). We expect that given any appropriate property ϕ, there is in fact an answer to the issue whether or not an object has ϕ (excluded middle). We draw a distinction between what people think and say about an object, and the facts (realism). And we think a true proposition about an object, will be true no matter who thinks or states it (objectivity).

These expectations reflect that fact that notion-networks developed in order to allow information to be accumulated about real objects and communicated to others—as an extension of what I've called the detach and recognize information game.

Now consider my belief that Socrates enjoyed philosophy. Assuming that this is accurate and a matter of knowledge or something like it and not just a lucky guess, there will be two different relations between this belief and Socrates. Socrates will be the origin of my notion, because of the etiological structure, which we imagine leads back from my notions to Durant's notions to Plato's perceptions and then to Socrates. But we can also start from the content, my association of my idea of liking philosophy with my Socrates notion. This association flowed to me from Durant via his writings, and to Durant from Plato via his writings. Its ultimate *source*, to use Evans's term, was Socrates, whose philosophy-loving behavior affected Plato's perceptions of him. Socrates then stands in two relations to my belief that he loved philosophy; he was the origin of the notion, and the source of the information. In this case, the etiology of the notion and the route of the flow of the information are essentially the same.

But now consider my belief that Socrates was pot-bellied. The source of this was Socrates, but the route was different. Xenophon probably saw that this was so himself (assuming his attribution is accurate). Chris Bobonich learned it by reading Xenophon, and he told me.

Thus there are two things associated in my head, the notion of Socrates, and the idea of his being pot-bellied, that arrived there by two different routes. In this case the etiology of the notion and the route of the flow of information are quite different.

If our system of notions and files is to be of any use to us, we must have the ability to keep things in fairly good order—that is, to keep information about a thing attached to our notion of that thing. That is, we not only need content in our files that will allow us to recognize the object the file is of, should we encounter it, we also need content that will allow us to recognize references to the object.

One version of descriptivism holds that a mental file is about the object that it best fits, its *denotation*. This may be based on several misconstrued insights. The first is that there must be some account of why a name designates the object it does. A second is that files without adequate recognition mechanisms are of no use to helping us in our encounters with the objects the files are about. Here then is a another point, that to pick up more information about the object through communication, we need to know enough about it to recognize references to it. None of these insights adds up to descriptivism; the last two confuse a condition files must meet to usefully designate an object with the condition they must meet to designate an object at all.

Another ideal is that the origin of our notion should also be the source of all of the information associated with the notion. It should at least be what Evans calls the 'dominant source' of that information. To the extent that the denotational and dominant source conditions are not met, the file becomes useless for helping guide behavior toward the object it is about.

Let's dub my Socrates notion *Soc*. Optimistically, we have

The origin of Soc = The dominant source of information associated with Soc = The denotation of Soc

I have appealed to the object the notion is *about* or *of*. This is the object whose properties determine the truth or falsity of the beliefs one has as a result of having a file in one's mind. When the relation of being the origin of the notion and the dominant source of the file coincide, that object is clearly the one that the notion is about. But there are all sorts of cases in which things are not so clear. In some cases there isn't a dominant source: through a series of misrecognitions, a file becomes a mess with different sources. Perhaps there is a dominant source, but it has changed over time due to a misrecognition that continued over a long period of time; the file has so to speak been stolen from its origin and taken over by another network. That is, a notion that itself has an origin becomes the systematic depository of content about some other object. In some cases, such as Santa Claus, a notion with an origin becomes a repository for fictional content, to an extent that overwhelms the historical content. When the denotation, origin, and dominant source are not the same, which object is the notion really a notion of? Evans would choose the dominant source (1973). The descriptivist tradition would choose the unique denotation or near-denotation. A historical-theorist might insist on the origin.

Given the classificatory concept of content, and a clear understanding of how these options usually fit together but can sometimes come apart, the question of which object a notion *really* is of, or which thing or person a use of a name *really* stands for, in a problematic situation, loses a good deal of its urgency. That said, I think the ideas behind Evans concept of 'dominant source' fit in well with the notion-network account. If a notion or a network of notions comes to be used for dealing with information about an object other than the original source, we have a case of co-option: a notion of one thing, with its associated file, is merged with another notion, creating a mess; but over time the result is clearly used to handle information about one of the alternative origins. One of the files has been co-opted: we actually a mess with multiple origins plus diversions. For example, the Saint Nicholas network was co-opted once or twice. The first candidate is when the notion of the child-friendly eighth century Turkish bishop was identified with the patron saint of children. But perhaps that was a correct identification, or perhaps it was merely a lot of religiously-based supersitition being added to the file of a real person. But then in the nineteenth and twentieth centuries Clement Moore, Thomas Nast, and the Coca-Cola Company commandeered this network, fictionalized it, and created our present Santa Claus, the patron saint of the commercialization of Christmas (*Encyclopedia Americana*, 1987). Evans provides a wonderful example, Madagascar (1973). A native told Marco Polo about 'Madagascar', by which the native meant the local part of the mainland of southeastern Africa. Polo mistakenly took him to be talking about the immense island off the mainland. Polo's reference buffer had the mainland as origin, for this was the origin of the native's notion that guided what he said to Polo. But Polo immediately merged this with his notion of the island off the mainland: a mess. So the Madagascar network that Europeans inherited from Polo began as a mess, but by co-option became a notion of the Island, supporting a new convention for the use of the term 'Madagascar'.

One might suppose that something less dramatic than co-option is going on. Except for the importance of the bit of misinformation added to his island file as a result of his conversation, being called 'Madagascar', there would be little temptation to think that the merging of the files changed which bit of land Polo's notion was about. It would be like my mistake of taking David Israel to be Paul Newman. On this account Polo's notion of the island continued to be of the island, and so too were the notions derived from his by iteration of (E2), (E3) and (E4). What changed was the name 'Madagascar'; it went from being mistakenly applied to the island to being a new name for the island, at some indefinite point when calling the island 'Madagascar' became an established convention.   Perhaps for the rest of my life I will claim that I saw Paul Newman in Palo Alto. But this one bit of misinformation does not make my Newman file about Israel.

8

The No-reference Problem

8.1 Introduction

In chapter 6 we looked at the problem of co-reference and names. The key ideas were that names were nambiguous; that most names answered to many conventions; and that the facts about the conventions in use provided a level of reflexive content that could do the work for names that indexical content did for pronouns. But in chapter 7, we saw that this machinery was not enough to deal with the no-reference problem. We introduced notion-networks and examined some of their properties. Notion-networks provide another layer of content: content given the connections of names and pronouns to networks, but abstracting from the origins of those networks. I'll now discuss these connections, introduce my candidate for *intentional content* and then use this concept to discuss the Jacob Horn case, and finally reflect a bit on history, fiction, and the various reasons we talk about individuals, present, past, and unreal.

8.2 Names, conventions and networks

Naming conventions are *supported* by notion-networks of the sort explored in chapter 7. The convention to call an individual a by the name α exists because in some number of people's minds a notion of a is associated with the idea of being called α. One way this happens is for a reference using the name to be the parent of the notion. A person hears or reads about Socrates, forms a notion of him, and associates the idea of being called 'Socrates' with it.

The number of people involved in supporting a convention can be small or large. My wife Frenchie has a cat named 'Microsoft', and William Gates has a company called 'Microsoft'. I'm afraid that even after this book is published, the number of people who have notions of Microsoft the cat and know his name will be small compared to the number who have notions of Microsoft the company and know its name. No doubt there are conventions that involve only one person and one notion: someone gives a name to a very personal object and doesn't tell anyone else about it.

Many conventions can reside in the same network. Cicero had three names; 'Tullius' was his clan name, 'Marcus' his given name, and he was called 'Cicero' because his ancestors were good at raising chick-peas.[39]

New naming conventions can come into being, with only indirect connections to the named object. The word English word 'Aristotle' doesn't look anything like the name that Aristotle's parents gave him, and probably doesn't sound all that much like it either. The same goes for the different sounding and looking names for him in other languages, such as the French 'Aristote'. These two names developed within the alphabetic and phonetic systems of English and French to give people a way of referring to Aristotle. People can still invent new names for Aristotle. Perhaps in an ancient philosophy class a beginning student asks a question about 'Ari-whats-it'. Soon everyone in class is calling Aristotle by his new name, 'Ariwhatsit'.

Above I said that an obstacle to our reflexive solution to the no-reference problem was that we didn't have an adequate concept of a naming convention. Now we will adopt a more complicated concept. A convention that governs the use of a name is a permissive convention that is supported by a notion-network; it permits one to use the name to refer to the origin of the notion-network. Where there is a block in the network, a name may be supported by a network with no origin, and so will

---

[39]Or possibly because one of them had a peculiar wart on his nose.

be an empty name, when used exploiting that convention.

We can now offer new candidates for the contents of (44), (45) and (46) more in line with our intuitions of contingency. We'll do this in two steps. First we have the reflexive contents:

(P^x44b) That **the network that supports the use of the name 'Jacob Horn' in (44)** has no origin (= ends in a block).

(P^x45b) That **the network that supports the use of the name 'Jacob Horn' in (45)** has an origin.

(P^x46b) That **the network that supports the use of the name 'Jacob Horn' in (46)** has an origin, and he was an important person in Colonial America.

Before pushing this further, let's review a bit of terminology. Early in the book the reflexive/incremental distinction pretty much lined up with the indexical/referential (or Content_M/Content_C) distinction. But there are actually several kinds of reflexive content — any kind of content that doesn't fix some of the relevant facts about the utterance. In the example of the obscure French philosopher and the note we considered a number of levels of reflexive content. Later, in discussing co-reference problems with names, we made use of content with the meaning of a name left unfixed. Finally, we've just looked at reflexive content where the network that supports the use of a name is left unfixed. Incremental contents, on the other hand, take all the relevant facts about the utterance as given; they are conditions on the rest of the world: what else, in addition to the linguistic and contextual facts about the utterance, has to be true for the utterance to be true. Referential content and designational content are both incremental in this sense, so we've had more than one kind of incremental content in our discussion.

There is now a new incremental level of content available in our theory, the level at which facts about networks, but not about origins, are loaded. Call the network that was begun with the writing of *The Horn Papers* 'N_{JH}'. Given that the uses of 'Jacob

Horn' in (44), (45) and (46) are supported by N_{JH}, we get three new candidates for the contingent contents:

(P44c)   That N_{JH} has no origin (= ends in a block).

(P45c)   That N_{JH} has an origin.

(P46c)   That N_{JH} has an origin, and he was an important person in Colonial America.

These propositions meet the intuitions of the last chapter. They are not about the utterances themselves; the first is contingently true, and the last two contingently false. So far they seem like good candidates for intentional content. Before we take this step, however, we need to look at the interactions of networks and pronouns.

8.3   Networks and pronouns

If we leave Kaplan's 'dthat' aside, it is natural to think of indexicals and demonstratives as having a more direct connection to the objects referred to than names. Indexicals seem to be tied to utterance-roles, and to refer to the occupants of those roles without the intervention of a network. To be sure, sometimes a notion that is part of such a network plays a clear role in motivating the use of an indexical. I may be interested in talking to a person because I think he is Elwood Fritchey, the well-known resort-owner. I say, "You are Elwood Fritchey." I am referring to the person I am talking to with 'you', whether or not I am correct in supposing him to be Elwood. I am referring to Elwood Fritchey, the origin of my Elwood network, with my use of 'Elwood,' whether or not I am right in supposing him to be the person to whom I am talking. So we might suppose that indexicals and demonstratives refer without the mediation of notion-networks, while names do not.

Here is another way to look at it, however, that allows for a more uniform theory into which the reasoning above can be incorporated. Think of my perception of Elwood as the first node of a network, with him as its origin. The perception leads by

(E-1) to a buffer. This is a rather short network. This buffer guides my use of 'you'. The use of an indexical connects to network, although to a much different sort of network than is typical for a name. The buffer provides part of the doxastic background for the directing intention. I believe I can refer someone by using 'you', because I believe I am talking to someone. The reference of my use of 'Elwood Fritchey', on the other hand, is determined by a much longer network of which the perception isn't a part. In this case, since I take the person I am talking to to be Elwood Fritchey, the buffer that supports my use of 'you' also feeds information into my notion of Elwood. My Elwood Fritchey notion has an informational relation to my perception of Elwood, but not an etiological one.

This approach is helpful with an example from chapter 1. We imagined a group waiting in Cordura 100 for the arrival of a computer scientist to help them in an algorithmic emergency. A tree scraped against the door, and someone said, "That's him" and someone else shouted towards the door, "Are you the computer scientist?" If we look at things in the way just suggested, we can see this as the formation of a short-lived notion-network, with a type-1 block, a perception mistakenly taken to be of a person. Of course, it might not be short-lived. Perhaps the aggressive tone of the second questioner was credited with scaring the timid computer scientist away. Perhaps the story is told and retold for years, and a scholarly tradition is built up around identifying the computer scientist who was there, knocked, got scared, and left. Here we have utterance-roles for 'you' and 'him', a network, but no origin.

To return to Elwood. Later I tell my friend about meeting him: "I met a man at a party who runs a fabulous resort in Wyoming," I say. "Does he let friends stay free?" she asks. Her 'he' is anaphorically linked to my use of 'a man'. But 'a man' is not a referring expression. I have not referred to any particular person; this is anticipatory anaphoric co-designation of the sort we allowed in (E-3) of the last chapter. My utterance, however, initiates a notion-network. You are referring to the origin of the notion that guides my utterance; you assume I met a man, and took him to be someone who ran a fabulous resort. You could sensibly reply, "I doubt that he runs a fabulous resort in Wyoming; he probably is the manager of a seedy motel, and was pulling your leg." You might even continue, "I'll bet you didn't meet him, I'll bet you just read about him." You are assuming that I am talking about someone, that a notion with some origin is guiding my utterance, however much the effects of duplicity, exaggeration, or poor memory may also be involved. Such chains of anaphoric co-designation are local parts of notion-networks.

The syntactic structure of a sentence also imposes constraints that require that various bits of an utterance pertain to the same individual. When I say, "Elwood wept," the syntactic structure assures that the person named 'Elwood' and the person doing the weeping are the same. Think of finding two bits of a note, one with 'Elwood' written on it, one with 'wept' written on it, amidst of mass of stuff that for some reason you must sort out. Finding the 'wept' piece, you form a buffer for the weeper; there is no referring expression on the note; the argument role of being the weeper in a weeping situation provokes this. Your partner finds the 'Elwood' piece, and forms the notion of the person named Elwood and thus referred to. When you discover that the physical pieces match perfectly, you learn that the person named Elwood and the (alleged) weeper are the same. The information that the weeper and the person named Elwood are the same was carried, in the original note, by the concatenation of the NP and the VP. If on the other hand, the piece your partner found that fit perfectly had the word 'Everyone' on it instead of 'Elwood', your little notion-network for the weeper would in effect be blocked. This suggests that by thinking of quantifiers as blocks in intra-sentence notion-networks we might find the way to incorporate the use of pronouns as bound variables into the theory. Developing this will have to await another occasion, however.

8.4 Networks and intentionality

Intentionality is a characteristic of psychological and linguistic phenomena that is often glossed as 'object-directedness' or 'aboutness'. The most straightforward way for a thought to be directed at an object is for it to involve a notion of that object, and the most straightforward way for an utterance to be directed at an an object is for it to contain a term that refers to the object. But intentionality is a kind of object-directedness that is less demanding than this. An intentional thought or utterance can be directed at an object that does not exist. The Greeks worshipped Zeus, Ponce de Leon searched for the Fountain of Youth; Anissa expects Santa Claus to bring her a present; many people thought Jacob Horn was an interesting fellow; Geach's Hob and Nob think about the same witch, even when there is no witch for them to think about (Geach, 1967).

Although none of these objects exist, in each case there is or was a robust notion-network that supports a variety of names and descriptions. In the case of the Greeks, Anissa, Ponce de Leon, some readers of the *The Horn Papers* and Hob and Nob, these notions are or were components of beliefs in the objects in question; Anissa believes in Santa Claus, and at least many Greeks, I suppose, believed in Zeus, Ponce de Leon believed there was a Fountain of Youth, many readers believed that Jacob Horn existed, and the whole town was soon talking about Hob's and Nob's witch.

Compare Anissa's expectation that Santa Claus will bring her gifts Christmas Eve with her expectation that her uncle Joe will bring her a glass of milk Christmas Eve. Each belief involves one of Anissa's notions. Each is a part of a larger notion-network. Assume that she hasn't seen her uncle Joe since she was too small to remember him. Then all of the ideas she has associated with each notion came from communication with others. In saying that Anissa expects Joe and Santa Claus, and that these are the same people her little brother Everett expects, and that Anissa expects the same Christmas Eve visitor that children all over

America expect, we say nothing the truth of which requires Santa Claus to exist. Our statements about what goes on in Anissa's mind, and in the mind of others who share her belief about Santa Claus, imply that that there is shared network with which all of these beliefs are, but it does not imply that this network has an origin, that Santa Claus exists. It even makes sense to say that the person Anissa expects is the same person that her sister Natasha no longer believes in, namely, Santa Claus; Natasha might say, "Well, I *don't* expect him."

Since Anissa's expectation about Santa Claus doesn't require that there be a Santa Claus, can we reason that her expectation about Joe doesn't really involve Joe? No. Both expectations are supported by networks, but the two networks differ in an important way. The Santa Claus network does not have an origin, and the uncle-Joe network does. This fact about the supporting networks cannot be read off from the events in Anissa's brain. Nevertheless it is a real, if external, difference between the expectations. We may speak, if we wish, of attitudes that are not only object-*directed*, but object-*involving*. Anissa's expectation about Santa Claus is object-directed; her expectation is part of a mental and social situation suited to track objects. Her expectation about Joe is object-involving; it's truth requires something of a real object. But this terminology is a bit dangerous, for it suggests that the difference is *in* Anissa; that there is something about her internal state in the latter case that somehow reaches out and incorporates the object. But the difference is external; the network that supports her Joe notion has an origin, the network that supports her Santa Claus notion does not.

From the fact that Anissa expects Santa Claus to come tonight, it follows that she expects someone to come tonight. But it does not follow there is someone such that she expects that person to come. The first inference is legitimated by the semantics of mental states and the way they work. Semantically, if the first expectation state is correct (Santa Claus shows up) the second will be too (Someone shows up). But also the first expectation will normally lead to the second, at least if the question arises in Anissa's mind. If she is asked whether she is expecting someone, she will answer "Yes." But of course, sad to say, it doesn't follow from the fact that Anissa has the expectation that Santa will come, so the second inference, the exportation, to the proposition that there is someone she expects to come, does not follow.

Now consider:

(47)   Santa Claus is coming here.

When Anissa says (47), standing in her living room, her remark has no referential content. There is no Santa Claus, so there is no proposition with Santa Claus as a constituent. But her remark does have content of some sort. It tells us what she expects to happen. We can report this content by saying,

(48)   Anissa said that Santa Claus is coming to her house tonight.

The embedded statement in my report and Anissa's statement do not have the same referential content, but they do have the same intentional content:

> Someone is the origin of N_{SC}, and he is coming to **Anissa's house**.

This suggests that intentional content captures the truth-conditions with meaning and network connections fixed.

Suppose now Anissa asks me who Kris Kringle is, and I respond,

(49)   Santa Claus is the same person as Kris Kringle.

Why should I say this? Setting aside the question whether it could be said to be true or correct, what do I hope to accomplish by it? I want Anissa's notions to be organized in such a way as to reflect that the network that supports the use of 'Kris Kringle' is the same one that supports her use of 'Santa Claus'. I could just tell her that, of course, but she would have no idea what I was talking about, and would doubtless not sit still long enough for me to explain networks, names, notions and the like. I don't want her to *believe* anything about networks and the like, I simply want her mind to reflect the sameness of the two networks. That is, I want her to have a belief the intentional content of which is,

(P^{I}49)   That $N_{SC} = N_{KK}$,

so I utter a statement with that intentional content.

It seems a bit harsh to say that I lie to bring about this result. Walton's concept of pretence gives a gentler verdict: in interacting with Anissa on this topic, I pretend that there is a Santa Claus, and talk as if there were. By doing so, I achieve the effect I was after. Anissa won't start expecting presents from Santa Claus and additional presents from Kris Kringle.

8.5   Narrow enough contents

There is an important difference between Anissa's expectation about Joe and her expectation about Santa Claus that emerges only at the level of the referential content of her expectations and statements expressing them. Anissa's expectation about Santa Claus has *no* referential content, because the name 'Santa Claus' is empty. Her expectation about Joe has the referential content that he will arrive in the evening. The one expectation has a connection to real events in the past and the future that the other one does not. The difference in connection is due to networks and the social phenomena that support them; it is a difference grounded in things external to Anissa's mind, but an important difference nevertheless.

It is important to keep in mind the *classificatory* concept of propositions and propositional attitude reports. The various contents of Anissa's expectations are not entities that she interacts with. They are abstract objects that we as users of the apparatus of the attitudes and as philosophical theorists use to classify her mental states. These classifications can be 'narrow' or 'broad'. That is, we can take more or less of the world around Anissa as given.

In the case of an assertion or a belief, contents will be or be closely related to truth-conditions: what conditions must the rest of the world fulfill, in order for the assertion or belief to be true? Content is *narrow* or *broad*, depending on how much we include in 'the rest of the world,' that is, what facts we take to be fixed and what we allow to vary. The paradigm case of broader versus narrower content is the difference between content$_C$ (referential content, in my terminology; attributive in Donnellan's) and content$_D$ (designational in my terminology, referential in Donnellan's). Take the assertion 'The author of *The Elm and The Expert* likes to sail'. If we don't take the fact of authorship as fixed, what else has to be the case for the assertion to be true?

That *the author of* **the Elm and the Expert** likes to sail.

This is the content$_C$; it is narrower compared to content$_D$, for less is fixed, more is allowed to vary.

If we fix the fact that Fodor is the author, then what else has to be the case in order for the assertion to be true?

That **Fodor** likes to sail.

This is the content$_D$. It is broader, because less is allowed to vary, more is fixed. Think of the metaphor of broadness as pertaining to the factual base that we fix before we ask what else has to be true. The more we fix, the less that varies, the broader the content.

But the assertion equally has other contents, as we have seen. It has intentional or network content, which is incremental (facts about the utterance and context are fixed). And it has all kinds of reflexive contents. As our example about the obscure French philosopher and the note suggested, we can fix less and less, getting narrower and narrower content.

Using narrow content — that is, the classification of linguistic and mental events and states by abstract objects that encode truth conditions with relatively little fixed — is appropriate when we are using contents as a way of understanding relatively local phenomena. If Santa doesn't come, and Joe doesn't come, Anissa will be disappointed. The fact that one expectation has, and the other lacks, referential content is irrelevant to explaining

Anissa's emotional life. The appropriate way to get a handle on an individual's expectations is the reflexive content of their beliefs, the *connected reflexive contents* of their statements (see above, 5.7). If Anissa says that Santa Claus didn't come as a way of explaining her disappointment, the relevant mental fact is that she has a notion of someone who she expected to come with gifts and didn't. It doesn't much matter, just in terms of explaining the disappointment, whether Santa Claus exists or whether lots of other kids believe in him and lots of adults talk about him. If I say that Anissa will be disappointed if she wakes up and thinks Santa Claus hasn't visited, it is the network, intentional level that is relevant. I am presupposing that you have a notion, I have a notion, and Anissa has a notion all tied to files of a man called 'Santa Claus' that brings gifts — files that differ, of course, in that Anissa's is full of straightforward beliefs, while yours and mine have something in the file to indicate that it has no origin, and that children have expectations about him that parents and other older relatives are supposed to take care of. In contrast, when I explain why I called Joe, and asked him why he didn't come when Anissa expected him, the referential level is relevant. The file associated with my Joe notion is being used to guide an interaction with its origin.

The classical tests for intentionality include failure of exportation and failure of substitution. Exportation means that we can't infer from the fact that Anissa expects Santa Claus that there is someone that she expects. Failure of substitution is the fact, or as some might say the appearance of the fact that, we can't infer from the fact that Anissa expects Santa to come that she expects Kris Kringle to come. She might not know that Santa and Kris Kringle are the same person.

The explanation of exportation belongs at the intentional level. The issue is less clear with substitution. We can explain Anissa's ignorance at the level of reflexive content. Having heard people talk about Kris Kringle, she has a Santa Claus notion and a Kris Kringle notion. What she lacks is a belief with the reflexive content that the two are of the same thing. This lack doesn't involve the other notions in the network, or the origin. Still, it might be more natural to supplement this explanation with one at the intentional level, in terms of two subnetworks of the same large Santa Claus/Kris Kringle network. Then content relative to fixing the subnetworks, but not fixing facts about what larger networks they are parts of, could be used to get at Anissa's ignorance. This would be narrower than network content, but broader than reflexive content; we could get at the shared ignorance of Anissa and Everett.

When we characterize a person's assertions or beliefs with content, we want to get at what the world has to be like for the assertions or beliefs to be true. If we fix too much we won't be able to distinguish what has to be true because of external factors unreflected in her mind, and what has to be true because of the way her mind is organized. This will be unhelpful, perhaps misleading, for the purpose of forming expectations of what a person will say or do or infer based on the contents of their assertions and mental states.

If we fix too little, we won't have a handle on how her mind is connected to other people's minds and to the world. These connections are usually important in the use we make of the attitudes, and so we explain things at the level of referential or intentional content. The emphasis on incremental, subject matter content in folk psychology and folk semantics shows the importance of these concerns. Our ways of describing minds and assertions evolved as a tool for explaining how people interact with the world, and with each other based on shared networks of information.

Earlier in chapter 2 I briefly mentioned the naturalistic approach to content that lies behind this work. The fundamental kinds of content are the informational content of events and the success conditions of actions. There is no information in any event, no way the rest of the world has to be for that event to have happened, except relative to constraints. The thermometer's being at '90' shows that the temperature is about 90 degrees wherever the thermometer is, *given* the laws about how mercury, heat, glass, and other things work. The most usual and useful ways of classifying the information also incorporate particular ways the constituents of the event are connected to other objects into what is taken as given, and so get us from reflexive to incremental information. That thermometer's being at 90 shows that it is about 90 degrees on the patio, *given* those laws about mercury and the rest, and also *given* that that thermometer is on the patio. This relatively broad content, with connections between the information carrying event an the objects in the world around it, is our usual way of dealing with information.

It is the relativity to laws and facts that allows for a narrower or broader base of things taken as given to use when we classify events by their informational content — by what the rest of the world has to be like for them to have occurred. This relativity carries over to all kinds of content, including mental content and linguistic content.

In supposing that there is a scientific basis for content, so that it can be a useful tool for a naturalistic and scientific understanding of minds, it seems to me we must accept some connection between content and causation as a working hypothesis. The basic idea is that if one's belief together with one's desire cause an action, then the results of the action should promote the satisfaction of the desire if the belief is true. The content that is needed to make this principle, or some more sophisticated descendant of it, work in a specific explanatory context must not fix facts that are unreflected in the mind. Elwood's Cicero and Tully notions may in fact have the same origin, but because this identity is unreflected in his mind, we lose explanatory power if we operate at a level of content at which it is fixed. For ordinary life, referential content works just fine most of the time. In cases of unreflected identities, unreal objects, and other such phenomena, common sense seems to handle a retreat to intentional content or reflexive content without much fuss. But there is plenty of narrower content available for those who need to delve deeper.[40]

8.6 Jacob Horn

Let's return to Donnellan's example about Jacob Horn. In the last chapter we noted that there are no subject matter contents for statements about Jacob Horn. But there are intentional contents. These account for the differences between the content of statements about Jacob Horn and statements using other empty names, or even the name Jacob Horn, as used in another hoax. If two people who have been reading the *Horn Papers* both say "Jacob Horn was certainly an interesting fellow," we will take them to have said the same thing. This judgement makes sense at the level of network content. Their statements are each true if the Jacob Horn network that their uses of the name exploit has an interesting fellow as its origin.

How about the statement that Jacob Horn doesn't exist? As we saw in the last chapter, it is natural to take existence and non-existence statements using proper names as telling us that the relevant networks do or do not have origins. If we say "Donnellan said that Jacob Horn did not exist," we are reporting Donnellan's remarks at the level of intentional content.

It seems odd, however, to suppose that existence statements like (44)

(44)   Jacob Horn does not exist

always fail to express a proposition when they are true. It would be odd if those who falsely say "George W. Bush does not exist" manage to say something, while those who truly say "Jacob Horn does not exist" do not. Can we suppose that in the case of existence statements, or at least some of them, the network *is* the subject matter, and the intentional content *is* the proposition expressed?

Consider

(50)   George W. Bush does not exist.

---

[40]For more on these issues see Perry and Israel, 1991, Perry, 1998b, Perry, 1986b and the items mentioned in footnote 4.

On a referential reading, (50) seems self-defeating. It if expresses a proposition, it is false. If it is true (we are inclined to say, a bit incoherently), it doesn't express a proposition. What could the speaker be getting at? The natural reading is at the intentional level: our network of George W. Bush notions, gleaned from television images, newspaper stories, and the like, has no origin. So the interpretation of existence statements and non-existence statements at the intentional level has an inviting prospect.

Suppose George W. Bush overheard (50) and protested,

(51)   I do exist

he would not seem to be making a remark about this network, but about himself. Shouldn't a referentialist suppose that 'George W. Bush does not exist' and 'I do exist,' said by George W. Bush, directly contradict one another? Similarly if I pointed at George W. and said, "He exists" it seems I would have said that the man himself exists, not that a network has an origin.

Even in these cases, we need to bring in intentional content to understand the transaction. What is Bush's plan? His directing intention is to refer to the speaker of (51) in virtue of using 'I', and so to refer to himself. But he also intends to contradict (50). He wants to do this, because he takes himself to be the origin of the network that supports the use of 'George W. Bush' in (50); he takes himself to be the George W. Bush whose existence is under discussion. His use of 'I' is linked to the use of 'George W. Bush' in a sort of semi-anaphoric way. The reference of his use of 'I' does not derive its reference from the earlier use of 'George W. Bush'. But the remark is inappropriate if the terms are not co-referential. He intends to be referring to the origin of the network that supports the use of his name.

Consider

(52)   George W. Bush might not exist

I think the ordinary use of this would be to express the epistemic possibility that the George W. Bush network might have no origin. It's the sort of thing that might be said by someone who feared a cadre of Republican industrialists who have control of the media and have created an illusion based on old pictures of George Bush senior and actors borrowed from Saturday night comedy shows.

In contrast, 'George W. Bush might not have existed' seems to have a clear referential and metaphysical reading. The possibility would be witnessed by a variety of worlds in which George W. is never born; among others: worlds in which the senior George Bush and Barbara Bush did not have this particular child, worlds in which the Bush clan never got started, worlds in which life never evolved on earth. This can be reconciled with a generally intentional reading of existence statements, however, if we suppose it comes to

$$\exists x(\text{Origin}, x, \mathbf{N}_{GWB})\&\text{Possibly}(\neg\exists y(y = x)))$$

A more straightforward intentional use is also possible, however: The postulator of the right-wing conspiracy has given up the view, and agreed there is a George W. She utters (52) to register that while she now believes in the existence Bush the younger, she also thinks her conspiracy theory wasn't crazy, or at least wasn't completely impossible.

These considerations seem to favor further consideration of the default/dominant theory of what is said, briefly considered at the end of chapter 7. It seems that our concept of what is said is simply too useful to be confined to referential content in all cases. Semantics makes available a system of contents, reflexive and incremental. We choose among them, pragmatically.

In the case of identity statements, the triviality (true or false) of the referential content triggers the default mechanism; the default, referential, candidate is trivial, so we look for something meatier at the intentional or reflexive level. The examples concerning Bush suggest the workings of such a default apparatus in the case of existence statements, where similar trivialities lurk at the referential level. In both cases, if the individuals exist, the referential level is still available to connect the contents of thought and discourse with the world.

Thus Elwood the paranoid says, "Bush does not exist." I turn to Bush and say, "he said you don't exist." Since Bush exists, I can use the default; Elwood has said something false about Bush. Elwood the investigator of literary hoaxes says, "Jacob Horn did not exist." You disagree sharply: "Jacob Horn did exist!" I am convinced by Elwood. If I report the interchange by saying you and Elwood directly disagreed, I implicitly appeal to intentional content; he thinks the network has no origin, you do. What I take you and Elwood to have said, and to disagree about, will depend on whether I think the network has an origin or not. But what I think will not be betrayed by my words. I can say, "So you think that Jacob Horn exists, and you think he does not exist." As with the issues of what notions are about and words refer to, the classificatory concept of content relieves us to a certain extent in providing definitive answers in every case to the issue of what is said.

8.7 Playing with names

It seems reasonably clear that, in some sense, the detach, share and recognize information game is at the core of our use of names. Names help us share and store information which is useful in actually dealing with the people, animals, things and places, named; in finding them and interacting with them if they are people or pets; in asking others about them and telling them what we know. It is hard, though not impossible, to imagine the practice evolving if it did not serve this purpose.

But this does not in itself imply much about how we use names. As an analogy, consider the evolution of our hands, with the long flexible fingers and opposed thumbs. Why did these hands evolve? Perhaps because they were good for ripping small animals apart, or dealing effectively with other hominoids? Probably not because they are well-suited for typing, playing the piano expressing thoughts, or throwing, catching, and trying to hit baseballs. Yet such things as these are what we value about our hands now. Relatively few of us spend much time ripping small animals apart, or pushing other hominoids out of our or their territories.

Similarly, names are parts of grand information games that have nothing to do with dealing directly with the people named, namely, history and fiction. Many of us love to read about dead people and people that never were, and love to write and talk to others about these things. Indeed, for some, perhaps the main reason we ever use language to help us directly interact with people is that it helps us spend the rest of our time dealing with the dead and non-existent. I talk with librarians, and hold office hours with students, because these interactions help me find books about Hume, recruit others to the wonderful institution of reading and thinking about dead philosophers, and pay the bills. Apart from that, interacting with real, live people is about as inviting as ripping small animals apart. (I exaggerate a bit here, for effect.)

The activities of typing, playing the piano, turning knobs on stereos, combing our hair, putting on make-up and the like are in no way dishonored by the fact that hands did not evolve for these uses, but for something rather more gross. Similarly, that history and fiction are relatively recent uses of name-notion-networks in no way diminishes their beauty or importance.

We can distinguish three ways we use names in discourse about reality: when directly interacting with the object, when indirectly interacting with the object, and in what I call *mere discourse*, discourse involving names that refer, where there is no possibility of direct interaction.

Names help us in our direct interactions with objects. They can help us find and recognize the object named. Names are used to label both inanimate and animate objects; some inanimate objects, like buildings, display their names prominently, while many dogs and humans and some other animate objects are taught to respond to their names.

Perhaps there was a sign 'Parthenon' on the Parthenon. It helped Athenians know which building it was. Suppose Thrasymachus knew that he has to go to the Parthenon. He had a notion of the Parthenon, and some ideas associated with it, such as, 'is the building where one applies for a permit to teach rhetoric.' He had never been to the Parthenon and didn't really know what it looked like. But he knew it was called 'Parthenon'. This is one of the ideas he associated with it. When he saw the sign, he knew he was at the right building.[41]

We also use tags with names on them for animate objects. Cats and dogs have tags on their collars, soldiers wear them around their necks, and philosophers sometimes wear them pinned to their shirts when they attend conferences. It would be convenient if people's names were permanently affixed to them—tattooed on the forehead, perhaps. But until this catches on we make do with temporary labels.

We also use names of people and animals to get their attention. Kaplan notes how handy the names of children are when it is time to call them home for dinner. Thrasymachus can use Socrates' name as a way of identifying him, even if he is not wearing a nametag. He may have heard of Socrates but never met him. Looking for an argument, he says "Socrates" loudly upon leaving the Parthenon with his license, and watches to see who responds.

People exchange content with other people who have inter-acted or will interact with objects in which they are interested. To do this they need to refer to the objects, and names are one way of doing this. Socrates' mother may tell teen-aged Xantippe, Socrates' future wife and widow, that Socrates is hanging around the Parthenon, so that Xantippe can go hang out with him. Socrates' mother and Xantippe both have notions of Socrates and more or less rich files on him. Socrates' mother shares content

---

[41]Philosophers sometimes use the term 'metalinguistic' for any knowledge or statement that involves language. On this usage, Thrasymachus's knowledge about the Parthenon's name is metalinguistic. I think this is an unfortunate usage. We don't call Thrasymachus's knowledge about what color the Parthenon was 'metacoloristic' knowledge. His knowledge about its name doesn't differ from his knowledge of its color in any of the ways suggested by 'meta'; it is not higher, later, less central or important.

with Xantippe, and she uses the name 'Socrates' to identify the person she is talking about. This is *indirect interaction*, the use of names as an aid to exchanging information which will be later used in an interaction with an object. When Xantippe learns of Socrates' whereabouts from his mother, she is not at that moment interacting with him, but she is getting information that will help her to do so.

We also use people's names in writing to them, and in writing about them. Socrates' mother might leave a note for Xantippe, "Socrates is hanging out near the Parthenon." I also include these among direct and indirect interactions.

When the object passes out of existence—the person dies, the building is destroyed, the event is over—there is no longer a possibility of direct or indirect interaction. But people still remain who have memories of it. The next generation interacts with those who remember, each succeeding generation interacts with members from former generations, and so networks grow and content is passed on. Texts endure, and new writings are based on written records and conversations. This is *mere discourse*; information exchanges using names where there is no possibility of direct interaction with the relevant object. More than two thousand years after Socrates' death, we still talk about him. We no longer interact with Socrates, but we interact with people who have notions of Socrates and beliefs about him, and with written materials about Socrates. Discourse about Socrates continues, because some people enjoy interacting with the written materials, producing new ones, and interacting with other who enjoy the same activities. Others find themselves in various situations— taking an ancient philosophy course, for example—where they must interact with these people. To do so successfully they need to themselves interact with the written materials and develop their own Socrates-files that agree with their teacher's or differ in defensible ways. Some of them end up enjoying it. So the conversation continues.

TABLE 6: NETWORKS AND INTERACTIONS

	Direct Interactions	Indirect Interactions	Blocked Path
Original Discourse	Yes	Yes	No
Mere Discourse	No	No	No
Fiction	No	No	Yes

TABLE 7: WHY TALK ABOUT THINGS?

	Better Interactions	Truth	Fun and/or Wisdom
Original Discourse	Yes	As Means to better interactions	Perhaps
Mere Discourse	No	As means to Fun and/or Wisdom	Yes
Fiction	No	No	Yes

The Logic of Discourse About Reality

In discourse about reality we assume the principles of non-contradiction and excluded middle. We also assume objectivity and realism. We are realistic in that we think that no amount of agreement on the matter of whether a had ϕ or not can entail that a had ϕ. There is a metaphysical gap between the truth about an issue and beliefs about it. Even if everyone agrees that Socrates was snub-nosed, he might not have been. These principles all follow from metaphysical principles that are hard to doubt. Things either have or don't have properties; they don't have them and not have them. And nothing about what an object is like follows from what its representations are like, for representations can be inaccurate. The correspondence between representation and object may be quite reliable, but it is not necessary.

We apply these same principles to mere discourse. Socrates was not both pot-bellied and not pot-bellied at the moment of his death, but he was one or the other. In principle, he could have no longer been pot-bellied, even if all the evidence we now have about the issue suggests that he still was. The longer a tradition of mere discourse continues, the more remote any direct interaction with the person or object itself becomes, the less punch these principles carry, and the more likely it is that the distinction between what our best-researched representations say a thing was like and what it was *really* like will seem academic. If there is no possibility of going beyond the texts, in determining whether or not Socrates slimmed down in prison, what real point is there in insisting on the distinction between the truth and the evidence? On insisting that the issue must have an answer? Our hanging onto the principles may have no real practical point beyond the crucial one of indicating that we take ourselves to be talking about reality and not fiction. Why do we care about true about persons and things when the possibility of interacting with them has passed? One reason is that we think that the truth of representation is an important virtue in representations even when the things the representations are about are gone. We think knowing the truth about objects in the world will help us in our interactions with other objects. Perhaps similar situations will arise in the future, and knowing the truth about the past will put us in a better position to anticipate the future.

Direct and indirect interactions with origins are then in some sense central to the whole institution of notion-networks, as an extension of the detach and recognize information game. From this perspective, empty names undermine the whole utility of notion-networks, to provide a way of communicating detached information, that is potentially useful in interactions of someone on the network.

So, from this perspective, empty names are to be avoided, and mere discourse, where the name is not empty but the origin can no longer hurt or help one in any way, seems a bit odd. But of course humans are more complicated than this perspective suggests. If we think of the history and fiction in libraries and bookstores, the dramas in theatres and on television, the consumption of news about those who live and exist by those who have no opportunity to interact with them directly or indirectly, and hours we spend telling stories and reminiscing about those who are dead, it seems likely that the amount of discourse that is either mere discourse or fiction matches or even exceeds the amount that involves direct or indirect interaction with an origin. We enjoy discourse too much to confine it cases where there is the possibility of interaction; we continue with mere discourse after people die and buildings crumble. Mere discourse is too much fun to be confined to real objects, so we invent fictional ones, and inaugurate name-notion-networks without origins.

The logic of fiction

In the case of fiction, we drop realism and completeness—the principle of excluded middle. No one supposes there is a truth to the matter of how many hairs Sherlock Holmes had on the back of his neck on his forty-fifth birthday, or whether Holmes's great-grandfather had more grandchildren than Moriarity's great-grandfather did.

Consistency usually makes for a better story. Obvious inconsistencies interfere with with our participation in the pretence that a piece of fiction is true. It may be a evidence to suspect an interpretation or reading of a novel that it attributes inconsistency; but it is not a demonstration that one or the other of the attributions is incorrect.

To deal with the semantics of fiction we need more than an account of empty names that allows statements that contain them to have meaning and content. We also need to distinguish between different standards of correctness, and recognize the sorts of attitudes that go along with fiction. The way I will use the terms, truth and fit are both species of correctness. Truth is a matter of correspondence to facts; *fit* is a matter of agreement with the contents canonical representations. On this usage, it is correct to say that Sherlock Holmes was a great detective, but not true. It is correct because it fits with the canonical representations, the body of fiction about Sherlock Holmes left by Conan Doyle. It is not true, because there was no such detective. Finally, we need a belief-like attitude. Something that can, like belief, arouse the emotions and passions, that can people to cry when they read Dickens, or admire Sherlock Holmes, or be disgusted with Raskolnikov, but which falls short of belief. Kendall Walton has developed a theory of pretense that fits this role well Walton, 1990. I'll call such attitudes 'p-beliefs'.

Consider a use of 'Sherlock Holmes'. There is a use of this name that was established by a permissive convention due to Conan Doyle. Virtually all uses of 'Sherlock Holmes' that we encounter are part of a network with no origin, that was begun by Doyle's free creation of a notion. Conan Doyle is dead, but he left behind a body of writing that serves as a canonical basis for correctness for p-beliefs. I don't know whether this body of writings is fully consistent; I doubt it on general principles, and I have heard that Holmes aficionados have many lists of contradictions or at least tensions in the corpus. In addition to this written material, there are screenplays by others based on Doyle's stories, screenplays by others based on his characters but not his stories (some of which have Holmes and Watson involved in World War II at about the same ages they were when they were involved in the nineteenth century events depicted in Doyle's stories).

It is clearly possible to think hard about the fictional events depicted in the Holmes stories; to become emotionally involved with the characters and events; to argue about what happened or must have happened or probably happened at various points in the stories, and so forth. In doing so we balk at pointless applications of excluded middle; if the answer to an issue that is not explicitly considered *matters* to the story, we can worry about it, but not if it obviously doesn't matter to the story or the character (How many cousins did Holmes' maternal grandmother have?). To a similar worry about Aristotle's grandmother, we might say that even if the matter was some importance, there is no way of

knowing. With Holmes, if the matter is of importance, if something in our appreciation of the story or characters depends on
us knowing, there should be a way; Conan Doyle should have
written something about it somewhere. If he didn't, the problem
isn't that there is no way of knowing but there is nothing to know.

There is then a family of pretence games involving readers,
interpreters, movie-goers, manuscripts, books, screenplays, films,
videos, and the like. Within such games we can plan utterances
with the intent of influencing p-beliefs, actions, and the like.

What are the contents of p-beliefs? The most incremental level
at which we can interpret such beliefs is at the intentional level,
relative to some notion-based or interpretable artifact standard
of correctness. In the course of a discussion about how Holmes
felt about Watson, where we clearly are discussing the original
stories, and not movies or novels by other authors based on
Doyle's characters, you tell me:

Holmes admired Watson's physical courage.

Your statement is clearly correct if there are statements in the
Doyle canon that say, or imply, that this is so, and none that
contradict it, or at least none of equal substance and importance
to those that assert it. You are not making a statement *about*
the canon; it is not the subject matter of your statement. You
are making a statement the network loaded content of which is
roughly:

The canonical sources for the network that support the
conventions governing the uses of 'Holmes' and 'Watson' this statement associate the idea of admiring with
the notions tied to those names.

In the Sherlock Holmes case, this basically requires that Conan
Doyle intended us to think that Holmes admired Watson; he said
so, or implied that this was so, in the corpus of writing we take to
be authoritative.

9

Conclusion

9.1 Introduction

The dialectic of chapter 1 went like this. The referentialist position
has strong intuitive arguments. But the descriptivist position has
strong objections to raise against it, the co-reference problem and
the no-reference problem. History was slightly uncooperative, in
that Frege and Russell forcefully state the no-reference and co-
reference problems for referentialism three-quarters of a century
before Donnellan, Kaplan, Kripke, Wettstein and others made the
reasons that favor referentialism clear.

In the rest of the book, I have argued for a referentialism of
sorts, on grounds that the co-reference and no-reference problems can be resolved by appeal to various kinds of reflexive
content, and alternative forms of incremental content. The problems have to do with our inability to characterize the knowledge
that motivates and the understanding that occurs in cases of communication with co-referential or empty names and indexicals. By
embracing not only referential content, but various forms of reflexive and network content, the referentialist can locate these bits
of knowledge. The referentialist, if he subscribes to the reflexive-
referential theory I have developed, can find the contents the
co-reference and no-reference problems call for. A referentialist
can given an account of the cognitive content of true identities
and statements with empty names.

9.2 Dialectical reversal?

One might reply that this is at best a Pyrrhic victory for referentialism. What is left of the original intuitions and excitement of the great texts of referentialism, if we allow that the proposition expressed is only the referential proposition as a sort of *default*; if we deny that the proposition expressed provides the cognitive content; if we allow that there is a respectable level at which the content of true identity statements is contingent? What is left of referentialism as a powerful semantic revolution, if the key concept, referential content, has to share the honors with other sorts of content, and is singled out for special attention and honor for only what sound like reasons grounded in facts about communication, information processing and pragmatics? What is left of referentialism, if being *what is said*, what is expressed, the propositional content of a statement, is more a pragmatic honorific than a cold semantical fact that falls out of the structure of 'counterfactual possibilities'?

Indeed, one might go on to argue that the dialectic I have followed is no more compelling than one which deploys the same ideas in favor of a defense of a Reichenbachian version of descriptivism. The theory developed in this book *could* be called the 'Reflexive-Descriptive' theory. In that dialectic the no-reference and co-reference problems would be arguments in favor of descriptivism; the intuitions called forth by the referentialists would be ultimately unconvincing arguments against descriptivism. The Reichenbachian descriptivist can allow—following remarks found in Frege's own texts—that a level of content individuated by individuals referred to, and not the modes of presentation with which we refer to them, is useful and perhaps even important for certain purposes. The considerations I have raised could have been put forward as finding a location for the referentialist insights about counterfactuals and possibility, within a descriptivist theory, rather than finding a location for descriptivist insights about cognitive content, within a referentialist theory.

But this very reversibility favors the reflexive-referential theory. As I said in the first chapter, I regard the referentialist-descriptivist debate more as a structure for explanation and exposition, rather than an issue to be decided. My inquiry has been to find a place for the insights of both sides, rather than to decide between them. If the reflexive-referential theory is successful, it should provide a basis for defending the insights of either approach, and criticizing the excesses of the other.

But does the reflexive-referential theory really provide that basis? Does it appreciate the insights of both sides, or miss them? I'll end by arguing for the first verdict, by looking at an influential text from each side: Frege's famous argument from the the first paragraph of 'Über Sinn und Bedeutung', and Kaplan's famous argument about Peter and Paul from 'Demonstratives'. In between these discussions, I'll take a look at the reflexive-referential theory from the point of view of Ken Taylor's 'psychologized Fregean'.

9.3 Frege's argument

Frege asks us to consider the difference between $'a = b'$ and $'a = a'$. The first is synthetic and a posteriori, the second analytic and a priori. So their informational or cognitive values are different. A reasonable semantical theory must provide us with an account of this difference.

Frege has three different accounts to consider. The first is very much like the referentialist account. This is the account delivered by the basic semantical theory of his *Begriffsschrift*, without the special treatment of identity he introduced in §8. On this account statements have conceptual contents, which are functions of the conceptual contents of their parts. The conceptual content of a singular term is the object it stands for, of a relation-term the relation it stands for. The contents of statements are neither the truth-values of Frege's later concept of bedeutung, nor the thoughts of his later level of sinn.[42] It's not clear exactly

---

[42]I simply use 'bedeuten' and 'sinn' as technical English words to translate Frege's 'Sinn' and 'Bedeutung'.

what they are, or how structured they are to be, or even that Frege's account in the *Begriffsschrift* manages to be clear and consistent about this. What is clear is that if '$a = b$' is true then the conceptual content of '$\phi(a)$' will be the same as the conceptual content of '$\phi(b)$'. So on this account, the conceptual content of '$a = b$', if true, is the conceptual content of '$a = a$'. This is the crucial problem the referentialist has with identity statements, so for our purposes this alternative models referentialism. The problem of co-reference seemed to Frege, both at the time of writing the *Begriffsschrift* and at the time of writing 'Über Sinn und Bedeutung', adequate reason for looking elsewhere.

The second candidate open to Frege is the theory of his *Begriffsschrift* including §8, where he adds a special treatment of identity statements to the theory of conceptual content: '$a = a$' has the content that the sign 'a' stands for the same thing as the sign 'a' itself, while '$a = b$' has the content that the sign 'a' stands for the same thing as the sign 'b'. These are different contents, different propositions, one about the sign 'a', the other about both signs, one analytic, the other not. In 'Über Sinn und Bedeutung' Frege objects to this theory because it gets the subject matter of the statements wrong. They are not statements about signs, they are statements about the things the signs stand for.

The third candidate is his theory of sinn and bedeutung. The bedeutungen of the two statements are the same, the truth-value True. But the difference in epistemic or cognitive value is not to be found at this level of content, but rather at the level of sinn. The sinne of the statements are functions not of the things the terms stand for, as in the first theory, nor of the terms themselves, as in the second, but of the modes of presentation associated with the terms by language. In the rest of 'Über Sinn und Bedeutung' Frege went on to develop this theory and apply it to a variety of phenomena; subsequently the theory has been a partial inspiration for a number of semantical systems.

Does Frege give us a reason to give up referentialism? Did he really have a reason for abandoning his *Begriffsschrift* theories?

He clearly has good reasons for not liking the final theory he came up with in the *Begriffsschrift*, with its ad hoc treatment of identity statements. One reason he doesn't mention, but clearly appreciated, is that the problem that was bothering him has to do with identity, not simply with identity statements. Consider the difference between '3 × 13 is not prime' and '39 is not prime'. The first is analytic given the meaning of '×' and 'prime'. The second, while true and necessary, does not seem to me to be analytic. If it is analytic, it is so relative to different rules. The proof of the first would be one step shorter than the proof of the second. Frege needed an account that provides a general solution to the general problem that '$\phi(a)$' and '$\phi(b)$' can differ in epistemic value or cognitive significance even if $a = b$, not simply a treatment of the special case of identity statements. His theory of sinn and bedeutung gave him this, and he immediately applies it to all sorts of other cases. For example, his theory in 'Über Sinn und Bedeutung' provides an explanation of the different cognitive significance of 'Cicero was a Roman orator' and 'Tully was a Roman orator' while his *Begriffsschrift* theory does not.

The objection he makes is that the theory of the *Begriffsschrift* gets the subject matter wrong. This is a good reason for rejecting the *Begriffsschrift* theory. But it is not a very good reason for adopting the sinn and bedeutung theory, which seems to lack a very clear concept of subject matter. It is this lack which leads to a certain difficulty in explaining Frege's answer to the question with which he begins 'Über Sinn und Bedeutung': What is identity asserted of? Objects, or names? Clearly not names. But is it asserted of objects? Then it seems that the complex of the objects and what is asserted of them ought to play some role in his theory—it ought to be *what is asserted* by the statement, *what is believed* by the person who sincerely asserts it, grasped by the person who understands it and so forth. But that role is played by thoughts (*Gedanke*), the sinne of full sentences, functions not of objects but of modes of presentation. Is identity then asserted of modes of presentation? The thought expressed by '$a = b$' seems to be that the sinne associated with 'a' and 'b' are sinne of the same bedeutung. But the sinne of 'a' and 'b' cannot be what *identity* is asserted of, since the sinne don't have to identical, for '$a = b$' to be true.

The theory that seems to fare the best, when all of the considerations brought to bear in the first paragraph are taken into account, is the original, unamended, unpublished theory of conceptual content.[43] Frege merely had to avoid the subject matter fallacy, a step that seems more plausible than giving up the whole category of subject matter. The semantical rules of Frege's unamended theory guarantee that '$a = b$' will be true only if 'a' and 'b' designate the same object. From this it follows that whatever conditions there are for being designated by a, and whatever conditions there are for being designated by b, are all met by the same object; that is to say, whatever modes of presentation language associates with 'a' and 'b', determine one and the same object. These conditions of truth for '$a = b$' are quite different from those for '$a = a$'. They follow from the semantics of *Begriffsschrift* for determining the conceptual content of statements, if we ignore the amendment of section 8. Anyone who understands the language will understand the different truth-conditions of '$a = a$' and '$a = b$'. Only the subject matter assumption, the idea that only the level of content that reflects what we are talking about can be considered in a theory of the understanding of statements, their informational content, and their epistemic status, could lead one to suppose that identity provides a problem for the unamended theory of conceptual content. Note that like the theory of sinn and bedeutung, the account based on these considerations is completely general. The same principles that account for the difference between '$3 \times 13 = 39$' and '$39 = 39$' will account for the difference between '3×13 is prime' and '39 is prime'.

As far as I can see, then, Frege's famous argument has no force against a version of referentialism that includes reflexive levels of content, and provides no reason for a version of descriptivism

---

[43]See 'Frege on Identity, Cognitive Value, and Subject Matter' (Perry, 2001b) for a more elaborate discussion and defense of this claim.

that excludes referential content from having a central role in semantics.

9.4 On being a (psychologized) Fregean

In 'Meaning, Reference and Cognitive Significance' (1995) Ken Taylor identifies three Fregean principles and uses them to provide an illuminating discussion of a fictional character he calls 'the psychologized Fregean'.

> The psychologized Fregean is not a historical figure, but a useful fiction. It is what we get when we attempt to build a psychologically realistic account of semantic competence which eschews Frege's Platonism /ldots and endorses [the three principles] as constraints on the semantics of public natural languages.'

The three principles are roughly, that if sentences are cognitively discernible a reasonable agent can believe what one of them expresses while rejecting what the other expresses; that the sentences will be cognitively discernible only if they are semantically discernible, and what he calls the cognitive constraint on reference determination:

> In an adequate theory of reference, mechanisms of reference determination will provide routes of epistemic access to referents.

The psychologized Fregean then has a certain conception of where cognition and language meet. The cognitive significance of a statement, the belief a competent speaker uses it to express, and the belief a competent listener or reader will take it to express, will be a belief *in* the same proposition than the statement *expresses*. As Taylor puts it

> the psychologized Fregean conception /ldotspresupposes that there are in the heads of individual speakers stable and recurring attitude contents, of a fine-grained character, which are expressed by the sentences of a shared language, believed now by one agent, now by another. (176)

Let's call the role for fine-grained attitude contents that is thus created 'Frege's need'. Can anything satisfy this need?

Taylor argues that we cannot find such attitude contents. The argument turns on the problem that a psychologized Fregean will have finding the right kind of propositions to fit the conception. The psychologized Fregean cannot, of course, be what Taylor calls a 'crude referentialist' and suppose that all semantics provides for simple statements involving names, indexicals and demonstratives are singular propositions. Nor can he be content with the 'Kaplan-Perry' strategy, which allows us to individuate cognitive significance in terms of character rather than (referential) content.[44] There are 'not enough characters to go around'. Taylor imagines a case in which two utterances of 'That coin is rare and valuable' have the same content and the same character, but where a competent language user could clearly accept the first and not the second.

The would-be psychological Fregean must retreat to a position Taylor calls 'Heracliteanism about propositional content':

No two sentence tokens express the same proposition

The reader will no doubt recognize something like the reflexive-referential theory here. We do not claim that no two utterances (or tokens) can *express* the same proposition, for we have followed the referentialists in suppose that what is expressed by such simple sentences as we have been studying are singular propositions. But we do claim that different utterances have different reflexive truth-conditions which can be captured in different reflexive contents, and that these contents are cognitively significant.

Even this Heraclitean view cannot save the Fregean picture, Taylor argues. He considers the example of a token of 'I am hungry now' that is written on a blackboard:

(53)   I am hungry now

A student might see the token at one time, say as it was being written by an obviously hungry teacher, and believe that the person who wrote (53) was hungry at the time (53) was written. She might see the same token the next day, and not believe this,

---

[44]See Kaplan, 1989a; Perry, 1977; Perry, 1979; Wettstein, 1986; Wettstein, 1991.

not knowing it was the same token. But the lumpy proposition she accepted at the earlier time,

(P^{x}53)   That *the person who wrote* (53) was hungry at *the time* (53) *was written.*

is the very one she rejects at the later time. In spite of our Heracliteanism we have not found something fine-grained enough for the purposes of the psychologized Fregean.

Taylor's criticism is directed against a precursor of the present account (Perry, 1998a) in which the difference between utterances and tokens was not emphasized. But the distinction doesn't help here. The utterance the student witnesses is the one that she sees a trace of the next day; unknown to her the chalk-marks on the blackboard are the result of the same utterance she saw the teacher make, when he created the token on the blackboard the day before. Moving from a singular proposition about tokens to one about utterances seems a bit more Heraclitean in spirit, but does not solve the problem; the student has two modes of presentation of the same utterance.

At this point we might formulate what I'll call 'Taylor's Principle':

No singular proposition can satisfy Frege's need

This seems right. As long as our candidate is a singular proposition, there will be different ways of cognizing it, for there will be different ways of thinking of the constituent of the singular proposition. And it will be conceivable for someone to cognize it in one way, but not in another, and as a result of that, to accept the proposition in one guise, but not the other.

Call the utterance in question *u*. Taylor's student will have two beliefs about *u*. One she would express in Kaplan-English with 'Dthat [The utterance I saw the teacher make by writing the token on the board yesterday] was made by someone who was hungry at the time it was made'; this has the content that *u* was made by someone who was hungry. The other belief she would express with 'Dthat[the utterance a trace of which I see on the board now] was made by someone who was not hungry'; this has the content that u was made by someone who was *not* hungry. So the contents of her beliefs about utterances are inconsistent, while her beliefs are in some sense internally consistent.

Nevertheless, I think my Heraclitean view can be of some help to one who is inclined towards being a psychological Fregean. On my view, it is not having beliefs *about* utterances (or beliefs) that solves the problem, but appeal to reflexive contents of beliefs and utterances. The student's two statements in Kaplan-English have the same referential content, but not the same reflexive content. Thus they can be motivated by different beliefs of the speaker, and can lead to different beliefs on the part of the competent hearer.

The reflexive-referential theory then does not propose to satisfy the Fregean need with a singular proposition that is both believed and asserted, *nor even with one that is both the reflexive content of a belief and the reflexive content of the statement that expresses the belief.* As we saw in the discussion of Austin in chapter 5, what we need to understand is the relation between the reflexive content of a statement and the reflexive content of the belief it expresses.

To see how this works, let's take another example. Suppose you need a stapler. I see a stapler on the desk, so I say

(54)   That's a stapler.

The belief I want to express is one I have before I utter (54). Its reflexive content *cannot* very well be that of (54); on a structural view the reflexive content of (54) doesn't in some sense really exist until I utter (54), for it is a proposition with that very utterance as a constituent, roughly:

(P^x54)   *The thing to which* the use of 'that' in (54) *directs attention* is a stapler.

Let's suppose my belief b that I have a stapler has the structure $H(n)$, where H is the idea of being a stapler and n is attached to my perception of the stapler (see above, 4.3). So the reflexive content of b is roughly

(P^{x}55)   *The object of the perception attached to* n is a stapler.

(P^{x}54) and (P^{x}55) are not the same. Their relation is that the notion n which is a constituent of (P^{x}55) governs the use of 'that' in (54), which is a constituent of (P^{x}54). The meaning of (54) allows the speaker to express the thought, about the object that the speaker is attending to, that it is a stapler. If I know the meaning of 'that is a stapler,' I *know how* to say something about an object I am perceiving. I know how to create an utterance whose subject will be the object I am looking at. This know-how does not require me to have conceptions of my own notions and perceptions. I do not need have a way of thinking about n or b or the perception attached to n. I don't need to think about n, but to have n.

A person's notions are things for which, like any other things in the world, he can have indefinitely many modes of presentation. But one can get by without modes of presentation of them just fine, except when doing philosophy. Unlike things in the world, the cognitive effect of one's beliefs and notions on the person does not depend on the modes of presentation he has on them, but on the fact that they are his. They're influence on his cognition is due to being part of the cognitive apparatus, not in virtue of having an effect via modes of presentation on the cognitive apparatus. Frege's need, as analyzed by the reflexive-referential theory at least, is not for a special kind of object for which there is only one mode of presentation, but for object for which modes of presentation are not intermediaries to cognitive effects. Our own ideas are such objects, and the reflexive-referential theory shows how they figure in the contents of our thoughts and utterances.

The contents of my belief and my utterance then meet at two points. If things go right, they will have the *same* referential content; the object I believe to be a stapler is the object I assert to be a stapler. I will achieve this result, by producing an utterance of the sort that has the same referential content as the belief I want to express and convey to you. I do this by producing an utterance that is about the object I am thinking about. I can do this because the word 'this' refers to the very object that the person who produces the word 'this' is attending to. Thus the second meeting place: given the connection of the utterance of 'this' to my notions, my statement is true only if the object to which I am attending is a stapler. This is, in the terminology of 5.7, the statement's *connected reflective content*.

It is important at this point to distinguish between having a belief that has a certain reflexive content and believing that content. When I believe that the object is a stapler, I believe the referential content of that we get from loading (P^x55) with the fact that the stapler is the object the perception attached to n is of. But I do not believe (P^x55). That proposition is the reflexive content of my belief, not what I believe. Similarly, when I utter (54) I do not say (P^x54). What I say is the singular proposition that we get from loading (P^x54) with the facts that I am the speaker and I am attending to that stapler.

The meeting place between cognitive and semantic content is then not so straightforward as Frege, or even the psychologized Frege, may have thought. It is not quite where the Kaplan-Perry theory put it, but not too far away either. The meanings (characters) of sentences suit them to express things about objects that play certain roles in the lives of the speakers. To communicate, speakers choose sentences that will allow their listeners to follow cognitive paths to objects that play certain roles in their lives. The sameness of the (singular) proposition believed by the speaker, expressed by the sincere speaker, and understood and believed by the credulous listener or reader is the result at which we (often) aim. The means of producing this result is producing an utterance that in a sense *creates* a almost common role for the object in both lives: the thing (the utterance I am producing/ the utterance I am hearing) is about, and from which the listener can reason to a more useful mode of presentation.

Whether this is a Fregean perspective, I am not sure, but it is surely a perspective that accepts, in the spirit of Frege, cognitive constraints on semantic theory.

9.5   Kaplan and direct reference

Three Pictures

At the beginning of 'Demonstratives', Kaplan provides two pictures, the Fregean Picture and his Direct Reference Picture. Each is a right triangle. At the lower left we have 'Language (singular term)', at the lower right 'Individual', and at the top of the triangle 'Propositional Component'.

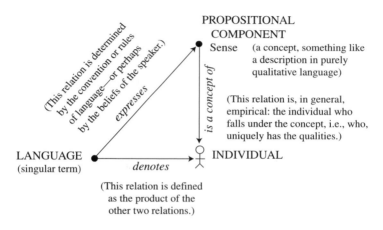

Fregean Picture

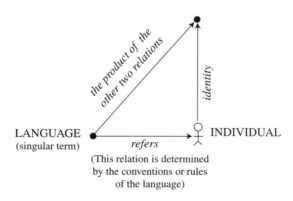

Direct Reference Picture

In the Fregean picture, the relation between the singular term and the propositional component is determined by the conventions of language.[45] The propositional component is a 'Sense (a concept, something like a description in purely qualitative language)'. The relation between the propositional component and the individual is that of uniquely falling under; that is, being the only individual who fits the sense. The relation between language and the individual along the bottom is labelled 'denotes' and Kaplan comments "This relation is defined as the product of the other two relations."

In the Direct Reference Picture, the direct relation, the one determined by the rules of language, is along the base and is called 'refers' and labelled 'This relation is determined by the conventions or rules of language. The relation between the individual and the propositional component (no longer with the comment 'sense') is identity. The relation between the singular term and the propositional component (the hypotenuse) is 'the product of the other two relations'.

With these two pictures in mind, it may be helpful to skip to parts 13-15 of Kaplan's recursive definition of truth and denotation in a context, in which he gives the rules for the denotations of 'dthat[α]', 'I' and 'here'. Let's start with 'I':

12. $[\text{I}]_{cftw} = c_A$

This rule gives the *character* of the English indexical 'I'. The character is a function from *contexts* to *contents* that models the rule English associates with this indexical. A context is a quadruple of agent or speaker, time, position and world. A sentence in a context is the semantical concept that corresponds to the speech-act concept of an utterance. That means we are to intuitively think of an utterance *of* a sentence, in a world, at a time, by a speaker, in a place or position, to understand how sentences in contexts work. The way we read this rule is:

---

[45]I ignore here the qualification'—or perhaps by the beliefs of the speaker'.

The denotation of 'I' taken (i) in the context c (ii) under the assignment f (iii) with respect to the time t and the world w is the *AGENT* of $c (= c_A)$.

This rule will give the same result, so long as the context is the same, no matter what variable assignment f or time or world we choose.

Suppose I say "I am now lazy" in the actual world on February 5, 2001 at 2 p.m. in Ojai, California. What has to be the case for this sentence taken in this context to be true in a world w? The person referred to 'I' must be lazy in w at the time referred to by 'now'. That is, according to rule 13, John Perry must be, for John Perry is the speaker of the utterance, and hence the agent in the context we use to model the utterance. So this seems right. Note that none of the other parts of the context were relevant to whom 'I' stands for, and neither are the time and the world of the circumstance of evaluation.

This rule then shows the sense in which Kaplan uses 'direct'. Kaplan is thinking of a Fregan sinn as something modelled by an *intension* in (classical) possible worlds semantics. In the simplest case, an intension for a singular term is a function from worlds to individuals. Kaplan is looking at it in a slightly less simple way, in which intension are functions from world-time pairs to individuals. A description like 'The president of the United States in February 2001' is nicely modelled as a function that gives us, for a world w, an individual that is president in w in February 2001. This would be a clear example of *indirect* reference. It fits the Fregean picture. Language directly associates an identifying condition, in my terminology, and language plus empirical facts (i.e., which world is actual) gives us the referent, namely Bush.

In the rule for 'I', the t and the w have nothing to do with what happens on the right hand side. The referent is determined completely by the context; it is c_A no matter what world or what time one chooses. So the 'propositional component' is determined once one determines c_A. In the example, the propositional component is me (or at any rate a constant function that always picks me) no matter what time and world pair we choose. This is the sense in which Kaplan's direct reference is direct —and it is the *only* sense in which it is direct. *That is, there is nothing about Kaplan's diagram that requires the mechanism of reference to be unmediated by the relation of fitting identifying conditions.*

This emerges quite clearly in the case of Kaplan's invented indexical 'dthat'. The rule is:

11. $|\text{dthat}[\alpha]|_{cftw} = |\alpha|_{c f_{c_T} c_W}$

As we discussed above in section 4.6, the idea of 'dthat' is that the object denoted by the description in the world and time of the context, is the object whose properties are relevant to the truth of what is said when evaluated in any world at any time. Suppose I ask now (February, 2001): "Does dthat[the present President of the U.S.] have a snake in his boots?"[46] The answer is "yes" with respect to a world w and a time t if George W. Bush has a snake in his boots in w at t. So the time and world *don't* matter, in this way: the time and world *of evaluation* don't matter. As we look at different world time pairs, it won't change whose boots we look for a snake in; it will always be George W.'s. But this doesn't mean that we don't have the mechanism of an individual fitting an identifying condition involved. George W. Bush qualifies as the referent of 'dthat[the present President of the U.S.] only because he is the unique person that has the identifying property *being the President of the U.S. at c_T in c_W*.

I do not mean that Kaplan is inconsistent. He uses 'directly' exactly the way he says he uses the word. It has to do with the step, or lack thereof, from propositional component to individual denoted. On the Fregean picture, there is a step, the step from sinn to bedeutung, mediated, typically, in possible worlds terms, by what the relevant world is like at the relevant time. On the direct reference picture there isn't a step at that point. One gets to the individual denoted independently of considering the world and time *relevant to the evaluation of the proposition as a whole.*

---

[46]The example is from Woody in *Toy Story*.

Reference is direct, even if in getting to the individual denoted, language doesn't directly give us and individual (in the ordinary sense of 'give us'), but instead gives us a function from worlds-time pairs to individuals (*being the President of the U.S. in w at t*) plus a specification of which world-time pair is relevant (dthat: 'use c_W and c_T').

Although Kaplan is not inconsistent, one might think that the diagram he gives us of his view is a bit misleading. The bottom line, from singular term to individual is straight and direct as can be, with no stops along the way. Is this fair, when he has in mind a process that involves, in the case of 'dthat', identifying who fits a complex property at a time? For that matter, is it fair in the case of 'I', where we have to identify who the speaker in a context is? Since Kaplan's concern is logic, he can consider contexts as simple n-tuples of elements, so that speaker is given rather directly. Still, the rule for 'I' is inspired by, and intended to illuminate, our actual practice in interpreting utterances, and in such cases the identification of the speaker or author of an utterance may be quite complex. The identifying condition, *being the speaker of the utterance* may not become a constituent of the proposition expressed, but it plays a significant role in the semantics.

We can fault the picture, but again, we can't really fault Kaplan. Directly below the Direct Reference picture he says,

(These pictures are not entirely accurate/*ldots*the relation marked 'refers' may already involve a kind of Fregean sense used to fix the referent)(486).

It seems that 'this kind of Fregean sense' in the case of 'dthat,' is the identifying condition associated by language with the description on which 'dthat' operates. In the case of indexicals, it seems to be the character. The direct reference picture theory, as Kaplan intends it, does not entail that the directly referential item is directly tied, by the conventions of language, to the object it designates. The essential thing is that, however indirect may be the route from meaning of the directly referential item to its semantic value, its propositional contribution, the step from that contribution to the object designated is direct. That is, it is either the step of identity (on the informal understanding of the theory, in which the propositional contribution is the object designated) or the step from an individual to a constant intension of it (on the theory as formally presented). If Kaplan is to be faulted, it is because his terminology of 'direct reference' and the diagram he uses to convey it are misleading, and more intuitive and memorable than his official explanations.

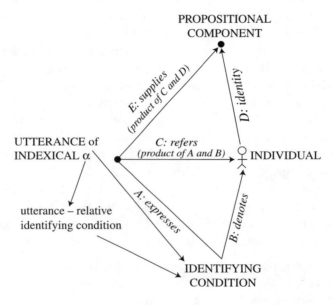

Combined Picture

We can construct a picture that comes closer to the letter of Kaplan's account of direct reference by combining modified version of the two pictures Kaplan provides. Start with the Fregean picture. Change the terms 'propositional component' in the upper right to 'identifying condition'. Then flip the diagram, and paste it on the bottom of the Direct Reference Picture. Cross out 'denotes' and leave 'refers'. Leave both glosses. So now we have a relation, called 'refers' between language and an individual, that is determined (in part) by the conventions or rules of language. The relation is the product of a connection between language and an identifying condition, and a relation between that condition and the individual. The individual is the proposition component, and this in virtue of the relations of reference and identity.

This combined picture seems to bring out the true difference between direct reference as Kaplan defines it, and Frege's view. Nothing in Kaplan's concept of 'directness' precludes the bottom triangle, the *indirect* route through something like a Fregean sinn to the individual referred to. And in fact his theory of character provides such a route. What is direct is the next step, from the individual to the propositional component.

9.6 Kaplan's arguments for direct reference

Kaplan's argument for direct reference comes in two parts, first an argument for pure indexicals, and then one for demonstratives. Kaplan says at the outset, 'I am *not* claiming, as has been claimed for proper names, that indexicals lack anything that might be called 'descriptive meaning'. (498) His point, in accord with what we have just seen, is rather that this descriptive meaning is not the propositional component.

His example for indexicals is

(56)   I do not exist.

The proposition expressed by (56), what is said, is the set of worlds in which Kaplan does not exist. It is not the set of worlds w such that the person who meets the condition of being the speaker of (56) in w does not exist in w. It doesn't seem like there would be any such worlds. It is rather the set of worlds w such that the speaker of (56) in the context we are considering—that is, Kaplan—does not exist. There are a lot of worlds like that — all the ones in which his parents didn't meet, or broke off their engagement, or opted for celibacy before conceiving the logician.

So the point of direct reference is simply that in *what is said*, the proposition expressed, that which I have called *official* content, puts a condition on Kaplan he is the subject matter, not the condition *being the speaker of* **(56)**.

The argument that demonstratives are directly referential goes like this:

> Suppose I point at Paul and say,
>
> [(57)] He now lives in Princeton, New Jersey.
>
> Call *what I said*—i.e, the content of my utterance, the proposition expressed—'Pat'. Is Pat true or false? True! Suppose that unbeknownst to me, Paul had moved to Santa Monica last week. Would Pat have then been true or false? False! Now, the tricky case: Suppose that Paul and Charles had each disguised themselves as the other and had switched places. If that had happened, *and* I had uttered as I did, then the proposition I *would have* expressed would have been false. But in that possible context the proposition I *would have* expressed is not Pat. That is easy to see because the proposition I *would have* expressed, had I pointed to Charles instead of Paul—call this proposition 'Mike'—not only *would have* been false but actually is false. Pat, I would claim, would still be true in the circumstances of the envisaged possible context provided that Paul—in whatever costume he appeared—were still residing in Princeton.(Kaplan, 1989a, 512–513)

Pat is a proposition with Paul as subject matter, Mike one with Charles as subject matter. These are quite different propositions. Kaplan is clearly relying on the robustness of our intuitions about the concept he identifies in three ways, as what he said, as the proposition he expressed, and as the content of his utterance. He thinks anyone should feel the intuitive pull of the claim that what he actually said was Pat, a proposition about Paul, but what he would have said had the context been different would have been Mike, a proposition about Charles. The argument seems successful to me. In particular, the proposition I call the reflexive content,

(P^x57)   That *the speaker of* **(57)** lives in Princeton, New Jersey

is *neither* what Kaplan actually said nor what he would have said had Paul and Charles tricked him.

There is nothing in either of these arguments with which the critical referentialist needs to disagree. The official content of (56) is a proposition about Kaplan, to the effect that he doesn't exist; the official content of (57) is a proposition about Paul, that he lives in Princeton.

Is there then anything about critical referentialism which which an advocate of Kaplan's theory of direct reference should disagree? That is, have these arguments given us any reason not to recognize, and recognize the explanatory importance of, contents other than official contents? There is nothing in these arguments to show that the official content, rather than the reflexive content, is the key to understanding the cognitive motivation and impact of the utterances. We would naturally retreat to the reflexive truth conditions to explain the oddity of (56) and the motivation for (57). (56) is odd because it is true only iff the speaker of (56) does not exist at the time (56) occurs. But the speaker of (56), at the time it occurs (though not necessarily later) is in an extremely favorable position to know that the speaker of (56) exists, for he himself is the speaker of it, the knowledge is needed right as he speaks it, and he knows that he exists. Kaplan presumably said (57) because he took the person he saw to be Paul, he thought that Paul lives in Princeton, he knew how to demonstrate the person he was seeing, and he knew that (57) would be true iff the person he was demonstrating as he said it lived in Princeton. A theory of direct reference provides no argument for ignoring reflexive content, and, properly understood, has no motivation for searching for such an argument.

9.7 Conclusion

I conclude, then, that the insights of Frege's first paragraph and the insights of direct reference are compatible, and the the account I have developed recognizes and incorporates all of them.

Suppose that Frege's distinction between sinn and bedeutung is no more than it is sometimes taken to be, simply the recognition of the difference between the thing a terms in a statement stand for, their subject matter, and the conditions in virtue of which those things are what the terms stand for. Then one could not, or at any rate should not, argue with this distinction or its importance. If acceptance of this distinction and its importance is all that is required to be Fregean, the reflexive-referential theory is surely Fregean. If this were all there were to Frege's theory, this book could have been written as a straightforward defense of it. But there is much more to Frege's theory than this. There is not only the first paragraph of his famous essay, but everything that comes later. There is an abandonment of the concept of subject matter, and an elaborate theory of sinn, that is inexplicable, I think, except on the assumption that Frege was taken in by the subject matter fallacy.

Suppose that the fundamental principle of referentialism is taken to be simply that in the paradigm conversational exchange it is information about the objects the terms stands for that we seek to convey, and that the various conditions those objects satisfy, the ways we refer to them and think of them, are not really part of what we say; suppose this and the reflexive-referential theory is a referentialist theory. I do not think that any more than this is required to interpret the letter of Kripke and Kaplan and Donnellan; this is mainly why I have couched this book as a qualified defense of referentialism. It is true that when many of us read their great works, and perhaps when they wrote them, there was a sense of greater significance for epistemology and metaphysics than this simple idea provides. Kaplan's use of 'direct', in spite of his careful explanations of his special sense for it, certainly fueled this mistake. If I am right, however, the rich implications for epistemology and metaphysics and other branches of philosophy, and indeed for cognitive science, can be appreciated only when we appreciate that there are two levels of explanation involved. There is the explanation of what our language is a tool to do, and the explanation of how it gets done on particular occasions. A great part of our language is devoted to helping us with our information game of detaching and recognizing—or better, detaching, storing, communicating, combining, improving, projecting and then recognizing and applying. Here the referential perspective is helpful, allowing us to focus on the detached representation. The referential focus mirrors the bent of many of our folk-psychological tools for classifying attitudes by their official, usually referential, content. I think this is pretty impossible to capture this part of the picture on the completely Fregean picture. But it is only half of the picture. There is also the issue of how our language helps with this information game; how on particular occasions the meanings of the words we have available to us helps us to store, combine, improve and communicate information in a way that allows it to be applied to the right objects. I think this is impossible to understand unless one adds a Fregean —in the more general sense— component to referentialism. Thus I have high ambitions for the epistemological and metaphysical insights provided by the reflective referential theory—for a stance we might call critical referentialism. This part of the argument was begun in *Knowledge, Possibility and Consciousness* and will be continued in *Meaning and the Self*.

Examples

(1) That man is a shabby pedagogue.

(2) I am a shabby pedagogue.

(3) Mach is a shabby pedagogue.

(4) I am a computer scientist.

(5) David Israel is a computer scientist.

(6) You are a computer scientist.

(7) Jim was born in Lincoln.

(8) The manager of Kinko's was born in the capital of Nebraska.

(9) Jim was born in the capital of Nebraska

(10) The manager of Kinko's was born in Lincoln.

(11) Ich! (said by several teenagers at camp in response to the question, 'Who would like some sauerkraut').

(12) I forgot how good beer tastes.

(13) I saw her duck under the table.

(14) Harold went into the Navy. He didn't like it.

(15) Percy went into the Army. He didn't like it.

(16) A woman wrote a very interesting dissertation at UCLA. She advocated subjective semantics.

(17) (Indicating a certain woman) She advocated subjective semantics in her UCLA dissertation.

(18) (Indicating a certain woman) She advocated subjective semantics in her UCLA dissertation.

(18a) It is raining

(18b) It is raining here

(19a) They are serving drinks at the local bar

(19b) They are serving drinks at the bar near here

(20) I am David Lewis.

(21) $\phi(\tau_1, \ldots, \tau_n)$

(22) $st[(\iota x)(Ez)sp(x, (22), z), (\iota z)(Ex)sp(x, (22), z)]$

(23) The house you live in

(24) The house you live in is quite attractive.

(25) You were born in the capital of Nebraska.

(26) You were born in Lincoln.

(27) I was born in Lincoln.

(28) 'This book is red' uttered by a speaker pointing at a certain book, located at coordinates x, y, z, t

(29) 'The book at coordinates x, y, z, t is red'

(30) That dog is that dog.

(31) That dog is not that dog

(32) this = this

(33) that = that

(34) this = that

(35) Smith believes that Harold is a spy

(36) I do not believe this = that

(37) Smith does not believe that this dog is that dog.

(38) David uses LISP

(39) David Isreal works at SRI.

(40) Paderewski is Paderewski

(41) Clinton likes hamburgers.

(42) Bill Clinton is taller than Hillary Clinton

(43) Bill Clinton is Bill Blythe

(44) Jacob Horn does not exist.

(45) Jacob Horn exists

(46) Jacob Horn was an important person in Colonial America

(47) Santa Claus is coming here

(48) Santa Claus is the same person as Kris Kringle.

(49) Santa Claus is coming here

(50) George W. Bush does not exist

(51) I do exist

(52) George W. Bush might not exist

(53) I am hungry now

(54) That's a stapler.

(56) I do not exist

(57) He now lives in Princeton, New Jersey.

References

Almog, Joseph, John Perry and Howard Wettstein, eds., 1989. *Themes From Kaplan*. New York: Oxford University Press.

Austin, David F., 1990. *What's the Meaning of 'This'?* Ithaca, Cornell University Press.

Barwise, Jon and John Perry, 1999. *Situations and Attitudes*. Cambridge: MIT-Bradford, 1983. Reprinted, Stanford: CSLI.

Burks, Arthur, 1949. Icon, Index and Symbol. *Philosophical and Phenomenological Research*, vol. IX: 673-689.

Castañeda, Hector-Neri, 1966. "He": A Study in the Logic of Self-Consciousness. *Ratio*, 8: 130-57.

Castañeda, Hector-Neri, 1967. Indicators and Quasi-Indicators. *American Philosophical Quarterly*, 4: 85-100.

Carnap, Rudolf, 1956. *Meaning and Necessity*, 2nd edition. Chicago: University of Chicago Press.

Church, Alonzo, 1956. *An Introduction to Mathematical Logic*. Princeton: Princeton University Press.

Condoravdi, Cleo and Mark Gawron, 1996. The Context Dependency of Impicit Arguments. In *Quantifiers, Deduction and Context*, eds., Makoto Kanazawa, Christopher Piñón, and Henriétte de Swart. Stanford: CSLI.

Corazza, Eros, 1995. *Reference, Contexte et Attitudes*. Paris-Montreal: Vrin-Bellarmin.

Crimmins, Mark and John Perry, 1989. The Prince and the Phone Booth: Reporting Puzzling Beliefs. *Journal of Philosophy* 86: 685-711. Reprinted in Perry, 2001a, Chapter 12.

Crimmins, Mark, 1992. *Talk About Beliefs*. Cambridge, Mass.: Bradford/MIT.

Donnellan, Keith, 1966. Reference and Definite Descriptions *Philosophical Review*, LXXV: 281-304.

Donnellan, Keith, 1970. Proper Names and Identifying Descriptions. *Synthese*, 21: 335-358.

Donnellan, Keith, 1974. Speaking of Nothing. *Philosophical Review* LXXXIII: 3-31.

Dretske, Fred, 1981. *Knowledge and the Flow of Information*. Cambridge: Bradford/MIT: Reprinted, Stanford: CSLI, 2000.

Encyclopedia Americana, 1987. 'Santa Claus'. Danbury Connecticut: Grolier. Volume 24: 238.

Evans, Gareth, 1973. The Causal Theory of Names. *Supplementary Proceedings of the Aristotelian Society*, 47: 187-208.

Evans, Gareth, 1981. Understanding Demonstratives. In Herman Parret and Jacques Bouveresse (eds.) *Meaning and Understanding*. Berlin and New York: Walter de Gruyter: 280-303.

Feigl, Herbert and Wilfrid Sellars, 1949. *Readings in Philosophical Analysis*. New York: Appleton-Century-Crofts.

Fodor, Jerry A., 1981. *Representations : philosophical essays on the foundations of cognitive science* Cambridge, Mass. : Bradford/MIT Press.

Frege, Gottlob, 1879. *Begriffsschrift, eine der arithmetischen nachgebildete Formelsprache des reinen Denkens*. Halle.

Frege, Gottlob, 1892. Über Sinn und Bedeutung. *Zeitschrift fü Philosophische Kritik*, NF 100, pp. 25-30. Reprinted in Frege, 1962: 40-65.

Frege, Gottlob, 1949. On Sense and Nominatum; translation of Frege, 1892 by Herbert Feigl, in Feigl & Sellars, 1949: 85-102.

Frege, Gottlob, 1960a. On Sense and Reference. In Frege, 1960: 56-78.

Frege, Gottlob, 1960b. *Translations From the Philosophical Writings of Gottlob Frege*. Edited and translated by Peter Geach and Max Black. Oxford: Basil Blackwell.

Frege, Gottlob, 1962. *Funktion, Begriff, Bedeutung: Fünf logische Studien*, collected and edited by Günther Patzig. Göttingen: Vandenhoeck & Ruprecht.

Frege, Gottlob, 1967a. The Thought: A Logical Inquiry. In *Philosophical Logic*, ed. P. F. Strawson. Oxford: Oxford University Press: 17-38. This translation, by A. M. and Marcelle Quinton, originally appeared in *Mind* 65 (1956): 289-311. The original, *Der Gedanke. Eine logische Untersuchung*, appeared in *Beiträge zur Philosophie des deutschen Idealismus* I (1918): 58-77.

Frege, Gottlob, 1967b. *Begriffsschrift, a formula language, modeled upon that of arithmetic, for pure thought*. Translation of Frege, 1879 by Stefan Bauer-Mengelberg, in van Heijenoort, 1967: 1-82.

French, Peter A., Theodore E. Uehuling, Jr., and Howard K. Wettstein, eds., 1979. *Contemporary Perspectives in the Philosophy of Language*. Minneapolis: University of Minnesota Press.

Geach, Peter, 1967. Intentional Identity. *Journal of Philosophy* 64: 627-632.

Heim, Irene and Angelika Kratzer, 1998. *Semantics in Generative Grammar*. Oxford: Blackwell Publishers.

Hintikka, Jaakko, 1998. *Models for Modalities*. Dordrecht: D. Reidel.

Israel, David and John Perry, 1990. 'What is Information?' In *Information, Language and Cognition*, edited by Philip Hanson, Vancouver: University of British Columbia Press: 1-19.

Israel, David and John Perry, 1991. Information and Architecture. In *Situation Theory and Its Applications, vol. 2*, edited by Jon Barwise, Jean Mark Gawron, Gordon Plotkin and Syun Tutiya, Stanford University: Center for the Study of Language and Information: 147-60.

Israel, David, John Perry and Syun Tutiya, 1993. Executions, Motivations and Accomplishments. *The Philosophical Review*: 515-40.

Kaplan, David, 1969. Quantifying In. In *Words and Objections*, ed. Donald Davidson and Jaakko Hintikka. Dordrecht: Reidel Publishing Company: 206-42.

Kaplan, David, 1979. Dthat. In French, et. al., 1979: 383-400. Reprinted in Yourgrau, 1990: 11-33.

Kaplan, David, 1979. On the logic of demonstratives. *The Journal of Philosophical Logic*, 8: 81-98. Reprinted in French, et. al., 1979: 401-412.

Kaplan, David, 1989a. Demonstratives. In Almog et al., 1989: 481-563.

Kaplan, David, 1989b. Afterthoughts. In Almog et al., 1989: 565-614.

Kaplan, David, 1990. Words. *Proceedings of the Aristotelian Society Supplementary Volumes* 64:93-119.

Kripke, Saul, 1963. Semantical Considerations on Modal Logic. In *Acta Philosophical Fennica*, Fasc. XVI: 83-94.

Kripke, Saul, 1979. A Puzzle about Belief. In *Meaning and Use*, ed. A. Margalit, 239–83. Dordrecht: Reidel.

Kripke, Saul, 1980. *Naming and Necessity*. Cambridge, Mass.: Harvard University Press.

Levy, David and Ken Olson, 1992. Types, Tokens and Templates. Report CSLI-92-169. Stanford: CSLI.

Mach, Ernst, 1914. *The Analysis of Sensations*, translated by C.M. Williams and Sydney Waterlow. Chicago & London: Open Court.

Marcus, Ruth Barcan, 1946. A Functional Calculus of the First Order Based on Strict Implication. *Journal of Symbolic Logic* 11: 1-16.

Marcus, Ruth Barcan, 1961. Modalities and Intensional Languages. *Synthese*: 303-322.

Marti, Genoveva, 1995. The Essence of Genuine Reference. *Journal of Philosophical Logic*, 24: 275-289.

Nunberg, Geoffrey, 1992. Two Kinds of Indexicality. In Chris Barker and David Dowty (eds.), *Proceedings of the Second Conference on Semantics and Linguistic Theory*. Columbus: Ohio State University: 283-301.

Nunberg, Geoffrey, 1993. Indexicality and Deixis. *Linguistics and Philosophy* 16:1-43.

Partee, Barbara, 1989. Binding Implicit Variables in Quantified Contexts. *Papers of the Chicago Linguistic Society*, 25: 342-365.

Perry, John, 1970. The Same *F*, *The Philosophical Review*, LXXIX, no. 2: 181-200.

Perry, John, 1977. Frege on Demonstratives. *Philosophical Review*, 86, no. 4: 474-97. Reprinted in Perry, 2000, Chapter 1.

Perry, John, 1979.The Problem of the Essential Indexical, *Noûs* 13, no. 1: 3-21. Reprinted in Perry, 2000, Chapter 2.

Perry, John, 1980. A Problem about Continued Belief. *Pacific Philosophical Quarterly* 61, no. 4: 317-22. Reprinted in Perry, 2000, Chapter 4.

Perry, John, 1986a. From Worlds to Situations. *Journal of Philosophical Logic* 15: 83-107. Reprinted Perry, 2000, Chapter 7.

Perry, John, 1986b. Circumstantial Attitudes and Benevolent Cognition. In *Language, Mind and Logic*, ed. J. Butterfield, 123-34. Cambridge: Cambridge University Press. Reprinted in Perry, 2000, Chapter 9.

Perry, John, 1988. Cognitive Significance and New Theories of Reference. *Noûs* 22:1-18. Also Report No. CSLI–88–109. Reprinted in Perry, 2000, Chapter 11.

Perry, John, 1990a. Self-Notions. *Logos*: 17-31.

Perry, John, 1990b. Individuals in Informational and Intentional Content. In Enrique Villaneueva (ed.) *Information, Semantics and Epistemology.* Cambridge: Basil Blackwell: 172-189. Reprinted in Perry, 2000, Chapter 13.

Perry, John, 1997a. Rip Van Winkle and Other Characters, *The European Review of Philosophy* 2: 13-40. Reprinted in Perry, 2000, Chapter 21.

Perry, John, 1997b. Indexicals and Demonstratives. In Robert Hale and Crispin Wright (eds.) *Companion to the Philosophy of Language.* Oxford: Basil Blackwell.

Perry, John, 1997c. Reflexivity, Indexicality and Names. In *Direct Reference, Indexicality and Proposition Attitudes* edited by Wofgang Kunne, Martin Anduschus, and Albert Newen. Stanford: CSLI. Reprinted in Perry, 2000, Chapter 20.

Perry, John, 1998a. Myself and I. In Marcelo Stamm, ed., *Philosophie in Synthetisher Absicht* (A festschrift for Dieter Heinrich), Stuttgart: Klett-Cotta: 83-103. Reprinted in Perry, 2000, Chapter 19.

Perry, John, 1998b. Broadening the Mind. Review of Jerry Fodor, *The Elm and The Expert. Philosophy and Phenomenological Research,* LVIII: 223-231. Reprinted in Perry, 2000, Chapter 17.

Perry, John, 2000. *The Problem of the Essential Indexical,* Expanded edition. Stanford: CSLI.

Perry, John, 2001a. *Knowledge, Possibility and Consciousness.* Cambridge: MIT.

Perry, John, 2001b. 'Frege on Identity, Cognitive Value, and Subject Matter.' In A. Newen, Nortmann, and R. Stuhlmann-Laeisz (eds.), *Building on Frege. New Essays about Sense, Content, and Concept,* Stanford: CSLI.

Perry, John, forthcoming. *Meaning and the Self.*

Perry, John and David Israel, 1991. Fodor and Psychological Explanation. In *Meaning and Mind,* ed. Barry Loewer and Georges Rey: 165-180. Oxford: Basil Blackwell. Reprinted in Perry, 2000, Chapter 14.

Reichenbach, Hans, 1947. *Elements of Symbolic Logic.* New York: The Free Press.

Russell, Bertrand, 1997. *The Problems of Philosophy.* Oxford: Oxford University Press. First published in 1912.

Recanati, Francois, 1993. *Direct Reference: From Language to Thought.* Oxford: Blackwells.

Salmon, Nathan, 1986. *Frege's Puzzle*. Cambridge, Mass.: MIT Press.

Smith, Quenton. The Multiple Uses of Indexicals. *Synthese* 78 (1989): 167-191.

Soames, Scott. 1989. Direct Reference and Propositional Attitudes. In Almog et al., 1989: 393-419.

Stalnaker, Robert, 1981. Indexical Belief. *Synthese* 49: 129-151.

Stalnaker, Robert, 1984. *Inquiry*. Cambridge: MIT/Bradford.

Stanley, Jason, 2000. Context and Logical Form *Linguistics and Philosophy* 23: 391-434.

Taylor, Kenneth A., 1993. On the Pragmatics of Mode of Reference Selection'. *Communication and Cognition* 26: 97-126.

Taylor, Kenneth A, 1995. Meaning, Reference and Cognitive Significance. *Mind and Language* 10: 129-180.

Vallee, Richard, 1996. Who Are We? *Canadian Journal of Philosophy* 26: 211-230.

Van Heikenoort, Jean, 1967. *From Frege to Gödel: A Source Book in Mathematical Logic, 1879-1931*. Cambridge: Harvard University Press.

Walton, Kendall, 1978. Fearing Fictions. *Journal of Philosophy* 75: 5-27.

Walton, Kendall, 1990. *Mimesis as make-believe : on the foundations of the representational arts*. Cambridge, Mass.: Harvard University Press.

Weitzman, Leora, 1989. *Propositional Identity and Structure in Frege*. Doctoral Dissertation, Stanford Philosophy Department.

Wettstein, Howard, 1986. Has Semantics Rested on a Mistake? *The Journal of Philosophy* LXXXIII, 4: 185-209. Reprinted in Wettstein, 1991, Chapter 9.

Wettstein, Howard, 1991. *Has Semantics Rested on a Mistake?* Stanford: Stanford University Press.

Wouk, Herman, 1951. *The Caine Mutiny*. New York: Little, Brown and Company.

Yourgrau, Palle (ed.), 1990. *Demonstratives*. Oxford: Oxford University Press.

Index

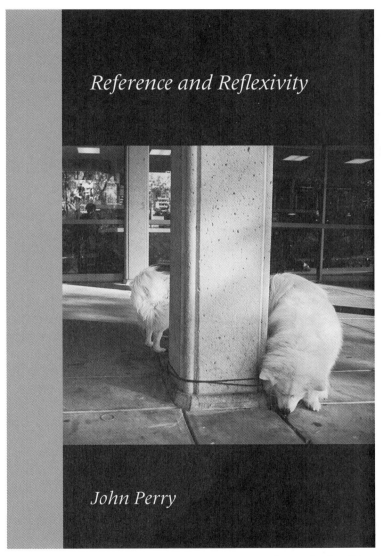

Reference and Reflexivity

John Perry

Front cover of paperback edition

In this book, John Perry develops a "reflexive-referential" account of indexicals, demonstratives and proper names. On these issues the philosophy of language in the twentieth century was shaped by two competing traditions, descriptivist and referentialist.

Oddly, the classic referentialist texts of the 1970s by Kripke, Donnellan, Kaplan and others were seemingly refuted almost a century earlier by co-reference and no-reference problems raised by Russell and Frege. Perry's theory, borrowing ideas from both traditions as well as from Burks and Reichenbach, diagnoses the problems as stemming from a fixation on a certain kind of content, coined referential or fully incremental.

Referentialist tradition is portrayed as holding that indexicals contribute content that involves individuals without identifying conditions on them; descriptivist tradition is portrayed as holding that referential content does not explain all of the identifying conditions conveyed by names and indexicals. Perry reveals a coherent and structured family of contents—from reflexive contents that place conditions on their actual utterance to fully incremental contents that place conditions only on the objects of reference—reconciling the legitimate insights of both traditions.

John Perry is Henry Waldgrave Stuart Professor of Philosophy at Stanford University.

Professor Merton French with the author

Cover photograph by Linda Cicero /
Stanford News Service

CSLI
PUBLICATIONS
Center for the Study of
Language and Information
Stanford, California

ISBN 1-57586-310-3

9 781575 863108

Back cover of paperback edition